EARN YOUR PIECE OF THE AMERICAN PIE

START YOUR OWN BUSINESS GUIDE

■ ■ ■

TAMMY MIHALIC

THE BUSINESS CREATOR

Earn Your Piece of the American Pie How-To Series: **Volume One**

Requests for use permission, speaking engagements, or any other inquiries should be submitted in writing at: www.tammymihalic.com.

Cover design and Illustration: Tammy Mihalic

Published by: Mihalic Publishing

ISBN: 978-1-956779-00-4 (Paperback)
ISBN: 978-1-956779-01-1 (EBook)
ISBN: 978-1-956779-02-8 (Hardback)
ISBN: 978-1-956779-03-5 (Audio)

Library of Congress Cataloging-in-Publication Data.

DISCLAIMER

This book is presented solely for educational and entertainment purposes. The author and publisher are not offering it as legal, accounting, or other professional services advice. While best efforts have been used in preparing this book, the author and publisher make no representations or warranties of any kind and assume no liabilities of any kind with respect to the accuracy or completeness of the contents and specifically disclaim any implied warranties of merchantability or fitness of use for a particular purpose. Neither the author nor the publisher shall be held liable or responsible to any person or entity with respect to any loss or incidental or consequential damages caused, or alleged to have been caused, directly or indirectly, by the information contained herein. Although the author and publisher have made every effort to ensure that the information was correct at publication time, the author and publisher do not assume and hereby disclaim any liability to any party for any loss, damage, or disruption caused by errors or omissions, whether such errors or omissions result from negligence, accident, or any other cause. Due to the constantly changing laws and regulations governing businesses, please contact your state's Secretary of State or the IRS.gov for the most up to date information about the laws that pertain to starting a business in your jurisdiction.

DEDICATION

This book is dedicated to my dear momma, who always had a dream to write, but never felt she could, and went to be with the Lord and never got to read my book. Bless her heart! And to you, the entrepreneurial reader, who will most definitely be bringing greater change to this experience we all share in called life. *Hold it! Value it! Love it! Cherish your freedoms to capitalize for all they are worth!*

MY MISSION

As a person who loves all people and their well-being, I want to give back by teaching people the steps they will need to take to easily start their own business to become financially independent and the benefits of having one while also eliminating some of the most common challenges.

Everyone deserves to have the opportunity to live the American Dream of owning their own business and take advantage of the many money-saving tax breaks that only business owners get. Everyone deserves the chance to create their legacy and a better life for themselves while cultivating happy experiences and providing income for themselves, their family, friends, and the communities in which they live.

My aim is to encourage and teach entrepreneurial skills and the secrets of the rich to everyone who wants to learn. *We make a difference, when we educate the world!*

It's never too late to earn your own piece of the American Pie!

Here's to growing our world, one successful business at a time!

CONTENTS

ENDORSEMENTS

"Wow! Impressive! This book really is an amazing tool for anyone looking for the easy, how-to steps to starting their own business. This is typical of Tammy, to go above and beyond to give you a wealth of inspirational knowledge. She loves helping people, and this book is proof! She has loaded this book with valuable, informative information that is crucial when starting out in business. It will definitely make your process easier than ever! This book is a must-have for the entrepreneur of any age and is the right tool you'll need to get your business started in a snap! As an entrepreneur myself, I highly recommend this book! It is inspirational, full of facts, and it shows you how to easily start your own business!"

- *Ron Rice, Havana Sun, Quality Suncare Cosmetics*

"This book is a great resource for anyone thinking about creating their own business. As a lifelong entrepreneur myself, it's exciting to see something fun and easy to read for new entrepreneurs. Tammy does an excellent job of taking you through the beginning stages of figuring out your business concept and leading you through incorporation and setup. She discusses important principles of management that many budding entrepreneurs overlook in the excitement of starting a new business. But most of all, she keeps it fun and positive, which makes this book very inspirational. I know you will enjoy reading and learning while feeling uplifted and motivated."

- *Tami Peavy, MBA, MPT, DPT, AIJ, Inc. and PTP, Inc.*

"Start a Business Without the Overwhelm! Would you love a business coach or advisor who could walk you through with ease the initial steps necessary to get your business up and running? If so, this book by Tammy Mihalic is your go-to resource for clear, concise, no-nonsense guidance. Tammy makes starting a business easy. She takes the guesswork out of all the maze of choices and reduces your stress by giving you access to the easiest methods—it's truly a 1-2-3-step system that anyone can follow and succeed! Her methods will shave off months of start-up time and save you money and time! I highly recommend this book."

- Lynn Kitchen, author, publisher and producer of World's Greatest Motivators TV Series

"I have known Tammy Mihalic for many years. This book is the embodiment of who she is. Tammy has created many businesses for herself, and has helped many others to do the same along the way. You can feel confident that this book will help you to accomplish your dream of starting your own business with ease."

- *Al Schultz, Enrolled Agent / Public Accountant*

FOREWORD

You know, in life, we all must come to that realization that it cannot be done well without earning a sufficient income! We need money to live a good life and to buy those things we need and want for ourselves or others. There are many ways of earning money in today's world, and one of the most lucrative ways is through self-employment. Unfortunately, many have no clue how to become self-employed. They haven't the faintest idea of how to determine what business they should start, much less how to get a business started. Nor do they understand the importance it holds when one is self-employed or how it will benefit their overall increase in wealth!

Working for yourself affects the entire quality of your life. It enables you to have financial freedom while helping those in your community. It's more than monetary. The reward of owning your own business is worth its weight in gold! Self-employed business owners are what legacies are made of!

In *Earn Your Piece of the American Pie,* my friend and student Tammy Mihalic has created for you an easy-to-follow guide to help you not only start your business, but she has also provided the easy-to-follow steps to help you make it legal. These easy-to-read steps will save you from all of the guesswork involved when you're just starting.

On top of that, she has given you a ton of great information that will not only help you decide what type of business may be right for you, but she has also, included multiple business ideas that you could easily start right from your own home. She has really gone above and beyond to make it easier than ever for anyone to earn their own piece of the American Pie!

As a self-employed business owner, she was able to add a lot of other valuable content to help you to complete the entire process of setting up your business... all the way down to your office setup.

She didn't just stop there either. She wanted to help ensure your success, so, she provided some very useful tax information and the beneficial deductions you are allowed to take just because you are a business owner. She discusses advertising and marketing strategies and the importance of customer care. She has even included the easy-to-follow steps in creating your company's service manual, which is a fabulous tool for operating your business.

As a business owner, Tammy knows just how stressed one can get when growing their business, so, she has made sure to include suggestions and ways to take care of yourself, both physically and mentally. So if you're considering starting a business as your main source of income or as a way to create additional income and the idea of owning a business sounds promising for you, then this book will have everything you need to create your business easily and effortlessly. It truly is a tool that will work for you.

I promise you will love just how easy she has made it for you to follow along. Your business will be up and operating before you know it! I wish you all the best with your business endeavors. And as Tammy says it best, "*Here's to growing our world, one successful business at a time!*"

- **Tom Antion, public speaker, lifelong entrepreneur, founder of Internet Marketing Training Center, and Screw the Commute podcast**

ACKNOWLEDGMENTS

I want to first thank God, Jesus Christ, and the Holy Spirit, who not only put so, many amazing people in my life but also gifted me with many skills, talents, and blessings. Without you, God, I am not sure where I'd be!

A BIG, SPECIAL thank you goes out to an extremely beautiful and talented person—my teacher, mentor, and friend Peggy McColl. Peggy, you have made a tremendously positive impact on my life. You have been enormously inspirational in guiding me into making my dreams come true. Without you, I do not know that I would have ever believed in my writing abilities, much less pursued them! One day, like you, I will be on the *New York Times* Bestsellers' list multiple times over and on stages all over the world, teaching my message. I love you, dear sister! I am so, happy and grateful I know you and have you in my life! ☺

A BIG, SPECIAL thank you to my friend and mentor Tom Antion. Tom, you encouraged me to find a way to help others and to give back, which led me to write this book. I am excited about helping others realize the American entrepreneurial dream of owning their own business here in the good ole' USA. Tom, thanks for sharing with me the mental skill your dad taught you—to always climb over obstacles that get in the way of our dreams.

Plus, a shout-out to Rick Frishman from Author 101 who introduced me to Tom.

I want to thank my friend Richard Anastasi who encouraged and motivated me to finish this book and brainstormed with me when I needed someone to talk to!

A thank you of appreciation to Joyce Walker who helped me with editing.

A BIG, thank you to Dorca Ochieng' for polishing up my final edit!

A special thank you goes out to Lynn Kitchen and Jared Rosen of DreamSculpt Publishing. Lynn, you are a kind and positive motivator. I am glad you are introducing some of the best motivators in the world to the masses! Jared, thank you for inspiring me to go beyond the business aspect of this book and for encouraging me to add more of my life experiences and stories so, that the reader may know me for who I am.

Thank you to all my friends and family who supported me in all of my entrepreneurial endeavors, including this book and the many more to come.

A BIG, SPECIAL thank you goes out to my father and mother. Mom and Dad, thank you! You instilled in me Godly principles, integral values, business skills, and a good work ethic. I am truly grateful for those qualities. I am so, happy and grateful that I was not only allowed to work with you both as I was growing up, but that you shared with me your own personal entrepreneurial opportunities. Those experiences are what gave me a creative edge and taught me to not be afraid of pursuing my business ventures. They taught me what it takes to be an entrepreneur, to believe in myself, to not give up, and to have faith when pursuing earning my own piece of the American Pie. For that, I love you even more!

A BIG, grateful thank you to Al Schultz for all of your input. I appreciate you!

A HUGE SHOUT-OUT to YOU, the reader. Thank you for trusting me to support, encourage, and help you on your entrepreneurial journey toward earning your own piece of the American pie! You are the reason I wrote this book.

PREFACE

YOUR FREEDOM AWAITS YOU

*E*arn *Your Piece of the American Pie* was created out of my desire to help people like you to become financially independent by becoming business owners. I was born an entrepreneur and have been self-employed my whole life, and would love to teach you. Owning your own business is my definition of owning a piece of the American Pie!

As a business owner, I have been asked the same two questions over and over again throughout my life: How do I go into business for myself? What do I need to do to get started? Of course, I am always happy to explain. However, I have been asked these common questions so, often that I began to reply, "One day, I should write a book!"

Then, out of nowhere, I kept hearing and being asked, "What are you contributing to society? What can you give back? What legacy will you leave behind?" I heard it so, often that I began asking myself what I could contribute or give back to people. That's when I thought, business! I can give people the steps they need to know so, they can easily start their own business and leave a legacy, share the secret of the rich, and how to live a good life! And voilà! I wrote this book for you, the aspiring entrepreneur.

So, what follows are the steps you need to take to easily start your own business and a secret of the rich! You'll also find many inspirational stories of how other entrepreneurs succeeded as well as a list of business ideas that you can easily start right from your own home! This book is a great tool for anyone wanting to start a business, if not today, in the future! The quotes and motivational stories from other entrepreneurs will not only inspire you but will inspire others you may know who also have a dream of being a self-employed business owner and independently wealthy. *Just imagine how good you will feel once you are living the American Dream of owning your own piece of the American Pie and having the money to buy those things you have always dreamed of owning!*

INTRODUCTION

HELLO, AND WELCOME!

I'm so, happy you're here. Congratulations! You are about to embark on a journey to earning your own piece of the American Pie! If you are holding this book, then it's not by accident! Your inner self is telling you to take control of your own destiny. Now is the time for you to fulfill that dream of owning your own business so, you can create your own empire of wealth! What is a business? A business is defined as any enterprise or entity through which a person sells, buys, exchanges, barters, deals, or represents the services or product offered in exchange for compensation. Owning your own business is one of the many ways to get rich!

I'm so, thrilled to be on this journey with you. I created this book to help you easily get started in realizing a piece of the American Entrepreneurial Dream. I will be giving you the easy, how-to steps, suggestions, and inspirational stories and quotes to motivate and inspire you as you create the business of your dreams!

Just imagine sitting back and reflecting on this moment three years from now, expressing how grateful you are that you bought this book and acted on your dream. You did it! You chose to believe in yourself and your dream. You're now leaving behind your legacy! You are well-known and a respected business owner in your city. Perhaps you have multiple employees and several vehicles on the road. You have made a positive difference in your community. You're even pondering the idea of franchising your gold mine, giving others the same opportunity, you've created for yourself. You're so, grateful you didn't let anything, including your own self-doubt, stop you. You went into business for yourself, and you can't even imagine what your life would've been like had you not!

Just think about that! How will owning your own business make you feel? Just imagine leaving your own legacy behind. How will it add more value, quality, and importance to your life? How will owning your own business give you that freedom you desire? Which dreams can now come true for you? Who will you be able to help in your family or community with the wealth you're creating? These are some of the important questions to ask yourself as we move along together that will help you to better understand your "why" you want to be in business for yourself, besides the large sums of money you will earn. So, stay excited! You're in charge of your life now! You are now on your way to earning your own piece of the American Pie!

"You don't have to see the whole staircase, just take the first step."
- Martin Luther King Jr.

In this book, I will lay out for you the initial easy-to-follow steps that you will need to get your business up and running legally. I'll discuss how to discover your business and name it. I'll lead you in the direction of success. Remember, I can only guide you in the direction of success. Only you can guarantee it by simply changing your mindset, applying your efforts, staying engaged, and be determined to overcome any obstacles that may get in the way of your success! Most importantly, like all things, **you must take action!**

I'll discuss the legalities that you'll need to know when starting a business, such as how to create the appropriate legal entity for your business, licensing, insurance, lowering taxes, and the tax deductions that only come with owning your own business. Did you know that you can write off any money you spend in pursuit of earning a profit?

I'll discuss easy ways to create the perfect office setup and share ways to stay organized. I'll cover marketing and selling tips, and how to bid your services to potential clients. I'll share simple ways of communicating with your customers to help ensure customer satisfaction. I'll give you tips on how to be more efficient with your time while operating your business. I will also discuss creating your business plan, along with showing you how to make a service manual for your company, which is a great operating tool for your business.

So, grab your highlighters, bookmark tabs, and writing tablets because I promise you'll want to take notes. In fact, make a folder to keep all of your notes in. They'll be a great reference tool for you as you begin to take your steps toward creating your new business. You can write notes on the pages of this book and highlight important information that you will want to reference later. I have also left you a page at the end of each chapter for additional notes.

Now, I want you to begin to imagine what your business will look like as you follow along with me in this book. Take time to dream about the perfect life you want to live. Write out your vision as thoughts come to you. Envision what you want to create, and display it where you can easily see and read it daily. Without a vision, we are lost! Remember, the Bible says it best, "As a man thinketh in his heart, so, is he!" Focus on and really feel the end results that you want to achieve in your life. Concentrate daily on the business you envision, the life you want to live, the legacy you want to leave behind. Proclaim, "It is happening! I am doing this! I am a prosperous business owner! My success is absolutely guaranteed!" Then discipline yourself, take action, stay in motion, be efficient with your time, stick to your task, be committed, stay focused, be determined, be driven, stay serious about your business, make it happen, and get it done!

"FEEL and IMAGINE the Excitement of having LOTS of MONEY and OWNING YOUR LIFE–DREAM!"

Please feel free to reach out to me if you have any questions or if you simply want to share your successful business-building journey. I truly want to hear all about your experiences!

If you find you need a more in-depth brainstorming session about starting your business, need coaching or have any questions, *I'm here to help you, from start to success.* I want you to succeed in your business and will guide you in whatever way I can. Please join me on Facebook, Instagram, Pinterest and LinkedIn. Join my email list to for New Releases and Products. I look forward to hearing from you!

"Here's to growing our world, one successful business at a time."

- Tammy Mihalic

1

WORK OR PLAY?

When you were growing up, did you ever play the fun board game Monopoly? How about another all-time favorite, The Game of Life, also known as Life. For those of you who haven't played, they're fun, family games that unknowingly teach players about economics and life skills!

The board game Monopoly was derived from the Landlord Game created in 1903 by a woman named Lizzie Magie. Lizzie was from the United States. She wanted to find a way to easily illustrate how the economy worked and to show it worked best when it was not monopolized by individuals, and everyone was allowed the freedom to create businesses and earn as much wealth as they could. With the game, she demonstrated that when people have the opportunity to be financially rewarded for their work, they promote the betterment of humanity and the economic growth for the country and the communities in which they live.

In general, Monopoly is about buying properties and developing them with houses or hotels, then charging rent to whoever lands on that property. It allows the owner of the property to earn income. The players learn how to become a business owner, operating as landlords and developers. They learn to buy, sell, rent, and collect rent money. The players also learn about borrowing money from banks, paying taxes, and paying their bills. The players quickly learn that they must take charge of accumulating wealth if they want to win!

They learn that there are consequences for not running their businesses or handling their finances properly. These consequences could mean losing it all, filing for bankruptcy, or having to go to jail! They learn there are rules to follow if they want to win the game! They also see how the community they operate in plays a huge part in the success of their businesses.

With the other game, Life, the player starts out by choosing to go to either college or get a job. If they choose to go to college, they take out a loan and attend school. However, if they chose to work, the player then picks a career and income card at random and plays by participating in real-life experiences such as getting married, having children, earning and borrowing money, buying a home, paying for insurance, taxes, vacations and so, forth. The game, in general, engages the player to learn about money-making careers, life experiences, and money management life skills so, that they can retire comfortably.

What I liked most about that game is it introduced the opportunity for players to imagine themselves in different career positions. I still remember, as a small child, looking at the fake money in my tiny hand after pulling the Rock Star card and the hundred-thousand-dollar income card. Then imaging how much money that was in real life as I traipsed around the world in jets and limousines, singing on stages while having fun. It was a career I could naturally relate to and see myself in. I thought about the skills involved when pulling any of the career cards. I thought about the money that could be earned and the talents needed to qualify for that career in real life. I was free to let my imagination run wild, and it did.You see, the fantastic thing about careers is you don't have to work for someone else to have one. You can have your own business within the field of work that you feel good in. You can be your own boss! That's what's great about living in America—we are a free enterprise country! We are allowed to create work for ourselves and reap a profit! Capitalizing on your hard work is why America is a great country to live in. We can grow, expand, and profit as much as we desire. Once you know what type of business you want to operate, you're set to go. This is the democracy of America and how you can earn a piece of the American Pie!

You can have as many businesses as you can handle. The sky is the limit! If you have the skill and motivation to meet the desires of people's needs and wants, then you have a platform to build a business on. People flock to businesses that provide a product or service that makes their lives better. Do you have the desire to enhance your skills and talents, giving people what they need and want? Can you be committed to your decisions and not back down when things seem tough? Life's results are ultimately made from the choices we make, so, choose wisely!

"Life is a game! How you play it will determine your success."
-Tammy Mihalic

DISCOVERING YOUR BUSINESS

Businesses are generally formed around a person's acquired skills, talents, passions, or interest. There are a lot of questions you can ask yourself to stimulate your inquiry into what business venture might be right for you. What natural gift or talent do you hold? Do you have a skill that could potentially be turned into a business, or do you want to learn a new skill? Are you working in a trade for someone else, and now you're ready to be in business for yourself? Can your gifts better our world? What careers motivate and inspire you? Do any relate to your gifts and talents? Can you see ways in which you can give back to your community with your skills? Do you see a need or want that needs to be fulfilled or a service that would give value to people's lives? Is there a trending economic need that you could turn into your business? Is the market already saturated with your business idea? Are there ways to make money with your idea? How can you make your idea better? How many people will want your product or service, and what will they be willing to pay? You may even consider looking at existing businesses that are for sale and see which ones you relate to. Plus, you could also consider buying into a franchise, or a Multi Leveling Marketing business.

Think also about the things that make you really happy! Is there an inner passion driving you? What in life are you truly passionate about? Is there a thing you really enjoy doing? What do you desire or value? What interests you? What amount of money are you looking to earn? What type of lifestyle do you want to live? What do you love about life? What service could you see yourself providing? What new skills are you willing to learn? What business can you see yourself operating? What work would you do even if you were not getting paid for it?

As you assess your strengths and interests, write them down, and then study your list. It's important to get a true understanding of your skills, gifts or talents, passions, and the trending market before starting any business. It will help you to better understand what type of career you're most attracted to naturally. It will show you existing jobs or services where you can apply your skills or talents or what new skills you will need to learn. This will help to reveal the type of life you want to live and the business you can build around it.

The key here is to find a business that you can identify with first, even if you may not feel you are qualified for that particular business. Remember, you can always learn a new skill, so, don't let learning something new stop you! Look for a business that is an expression of you. Pick a business that has your name written all over it.

Search out business opportunities that you can actually relate to easily. It is kind of like picking the right spouse to share your life with, so, you will want to make sure you'll be happy with your pick for the long haul. Divorce comes with a price; much higher than the cost of getting married, so, choose wisely and be very observant of your intuition, before deciding upon your profession. Carefully take notice of what type of business you connect to. Is there one that really excites you or makes your heart go zing? And most importantly, take time to pray and meditate on what business is best for you. *Whatsoever ye do, work heartily, as unto the Lord, and not unto man. Colossians 3:2.* Once you have the right business, it will be easy to build your life around that business and flourish.

"Every business is a service for hire that is scaled to a person's personal needs, wants, or desires."
- Tammy Mihalic

Before going any further, I would like you to take some time here to answer those questions. Take time to reflect on what businesses you may want to be involved in. Take a few minutes to reread the questions. Then stop, close your eyes, and imagine what type of businesses you could really see yourself loving to do! Do this for about ten minutes. Which business makes you feel really good?

As a child, I was naturally great with my hands and extremely artistic. Creativity was my middle name. Creating and building things came naturally to me. If I was in the creek, I would build a dam. If you put me in the woods, I would build a clubhouse. If I was handed clay, I would sculpt it into something useful. When I was allowed in the kitchen, I would create a delicious dish. If you gave me paper and pen, I would draw, transform its shape, or write a story.

Later, as life would have it, my gifts actually contributed to substantial financial gains, all from my passions for creating and building early on. I gained my first knowledge from building a cabin-style clubhouse out of fallen and cut down trees. That was followed by my experiences at construction sites and a hands-on vocational course on construction that I attended just for fun in high school. These were some of my talents and passions being utilized.

Early on in life, I realize I was good with people and speaking to them. I was very social and talked to everyone. I also enjoyed cleaning and making things look new. I found it a joy to transform a dirty home into a clean one. I enjoyed cleaning so, much that I started a cleaning business when I was eight years old. I walked door-to-door, selling my services. Later on, that passion turned into a very profitable business for me for many years.

I attribute my ability to be handy and figuring things out, inside and outside the home, from helping my father and mother as a child.

I did things like plastering walls, fixing trim, painting, refinishing furniture, building and hanging shelves, mending screens, and replacing faucet washers and toilet guts. I learned these simple skills because I was allowed to help my parents. Later, after being influenced by my grandfather, those skills led me to run a profitable handyman business right out of high school.

It's quite remarkable how the skills we learn early in life can actually become the things that bring us great wealth, makes us lots of money, and brings true fulfillment into our lives. It's all about connecting to our inner self and bringing it to life without judgment, trusting and believing in ourselves, and taking action. Isn't it time for you to design a life that you'll love to live?

Say you naturally are aware of the nutritional values in the foods you eat. You're even really good at growing produce. Some even say you have a green thumb. You simply relate to healthy food. You even have the ability to prepare good food and easily make remarkable meals but you haven't taken a cooking lesson in your life!

With a natural gift around food, you could easily become a restaurant owner. You could be the head chef who creates all the recipes for your hired cooks to follow. You only cook on holidays or special occasions. Your place is so, good that it becomes the talk of the town!

Perhaps your interest is in making and selling fully prepared dinners right from your own kitchen, cooking foods for everyone to enjoy. Or maybe you could create a unique niche' where you prepare meals for the elderly on particular diets or for diabetic patients. Maybe you have more of a sweet tooth, and making healthy desserts is more your taste, and you make and sell them right from your home. Or perhaps you would rather shop for all of the ingredients needed for a few meals and create a meal delivery service where you deliver the ingredients and recipes, and your customers cook it themselves.

Maybe you'll take your unique talents and have some fun creating a food truck business that travels to all the hot spots in town! The carnival atmosphere brings excitement to your bones! The idea of all those people enjoying your food is invigorating!

Maybe catering suits your fancy. You love the idea of attending parties and events. The thought of receiving all the compliments while serving your delicious homemade food excites you.

You could also advance your studies and become a certified nutritionist or health coach! You feel complete with the thought of helping others in your community to eat well and take care of their bodies. You love the idea of educating people about their bodies and their nutritional needs!

Perhaps, you would prefer to create a charitable food kitchen and find volunteers who will help you cook nutritious meals for the homeless or those in need of a helping hand. Your interest is more about serving than getting paid. It's your way of giving back to your community! However, did you know that as a charitable organization, you can still earn a salary while doing what you love?

You could go into the business of growing and selling organic produce at your local farmers' market or create a roadside produce stand. You could also deliver or ship the produce to your customers. The idea of working in a garden and tending to produce is rewarding. You love knowing you're bringing healthy, chemical-free foods to other people's tables!

Do you see how one's natural ability around food has the potential to become so, many different businesses? All you need to do is think outside the box!

I once heard about a woman who had worked at a factory for several years but had grown miserable with her job. She wanted a career change but was scared to make the change and wasn't sure what she wanted to do. She only knew she was no longer happy with her current employment.

One day, while in a session with her newly hired life coach, she explained her unhappiness and need for a career change. Her coach asked her what it was that she really loved. The woman replied, "I really love flowers!" The coach then asked, "What about flowers do you really love?" The woman said, "Besides the flowers being so, beautiful and aromatic, they are absolutely stunningly beautiful in a hanging basket!" She loved seeing them in hanging baskets so, much that she was making them for her own home on her days off and had them hanging all over her house. She also made them as gifts for friends and family. She believed that they brought joy to everyone who could see them! The coach then asked, "Could your love of making flower baskets be turned into a business? Would others enjoy your flower baskets as much as you do?" After much thought, the woman believed that others would love her flower baskets as much as she did. She believed it could be a terrific business to start!

So, taking a brave step out of her comfort zone, she started a flower basket business. At first, she only worked the weekends while maintaining her factory position during the week. Eventually, her weekend business was blooming out of control. Not only did she get to quit her factory job and work full time on her new flower basket business, but her husband got to quit his job too!

Today she owns and runs a hugely successful flower basket business that brings in over six figures every year. Wow! Isn't that amazing? Her love for flower baskets became the source of income for her and her family. Plus, let's not forget, due to her company's growth, she now provides employment for well over two dozen other people and their families in her community.

Her business all started with what she loved, followed by making a brave decision to turn her gifts and passions into a business.

Recently I heard of another plant lover who started growing indoor plants in her home and then created a plant delivery service for people who don't want to go shopping for plants. She simply uploads a picture of what she's selling on her Instagram and Facebook page first. Then, at no cost to her besides time, she posts them for sale on selling apps in her community like OfferUp, Craigslist, Facebook Marketplace, and Nextdoor. Then for a fee delivers them directly to the customer.

Are you a dog lover? Would you rather be around dogs than people? Do you and dogs simply relate? Are dogs attracted to you everywhere you go? Perhaps you feel the need to touch and adore every dog you see? Well then, you may be the perfect groomer if you are great with cutting nails and hair, cleaning ears and teeth, and giving baths. This could be the business for you!

Perhaps walking them or sitting for them is more relatable. You love the idea of waking up early and walking dogs in the crisp morning air as the sun comes up. You take great honor in taking care of dogs while their owners are at work or away on vacation. You've even considered extending your services to include gathering their mail and looking after their home.

Do you have a big house and yard? Then creating a dog hotel may be the way to go! Pet owners are always looking for places to keep their pets when they go to their day jobs or when they go away on business or vacation. So, why not provide them with this special service? You'd need an environment with a controlled atmosphere, a fenced-in yard, kennel space, clean blankets and bedding, clean food and water bowls, lots of newspaper and pee pads, fresh dog food and treats, and plenty of toys to keep the pets active. This is a fun business you could run right out of your own home. Just make sure all the pets have had their vaccinations and are not aggressive so, you can keep everyone safe! Dog services are a huge business that has risen out of people's love for their pets. Do you see how easy it is to take a passion or a love for something and turn it into a business?

Still not sure what business is best suited for you? Let me help by suggesting you take the Myers-Briggs Type Indicator Assessment. It's a fun, short test that will help you better understand yourself and your natural character traits, strengths, and weaknesses. The results of this test will help you understand what you're really like, how you respond to situations, and what people or job types are most compatible with you.

Having a better understanding of your personality type can help you discover what types of businesses might best fit your personality and the gifts and talents you have. This test can also improve how you interact with people at your workplace when you consider their personality type and your own. You'll learn to better interact with people like your customers, your suppliers, and your employees.

For more information about the assessment and how to get yours for free, go to: www.personalityperfect.com. I found their site to be spot-on and most helpful.

The test offers informative insight on the following: *Work and Career, Romance, Friendships, Parenting, Family, Life Purpose, Personal Growth, Daily Interaction.*

"Two things define your personality—the way you manage things when you have nothing and the way you manage things when you have everything."
- Unknown

What are your business ideas? Which ones can you really relate too?
Which ones do you really love?

_____

_____

_____

_____

_____

_____

_____

_____

_____

_____

_____

_____

_____

_____

_____

_____

_____

_____

_____

_____

_____

_____

_____

_____

_____

_____

_____

2

GETTING STARTED IS EASY

As an advocate for the self-employed business owner, it is my duty to all Americans and the world to write this book for our future generation of business owners. I am not sure if you knew this, but everyone should have some form of self-employment. It's true! Even if you are employed by someone else, you should still have a gig of your own. In fact, many start that way! The perks and tax breaks alone are very beneficial to one's overall source of financial increase. Not only can you operate your business from your home, but you can also deduct a percentage of those home expenses from your taxes that you could never deduct as an employee working for someone else. Tax deductions are the secret of the rich! Did you know that when you qualify and operate your business from your home, you could be entitled to as much as $1500 or more of yearly tax deductions?

They say getting a new business started is the hardest part, but that is only true if you don't know what to do. Getting started in business is easier than you might think, and I'll show you just how easy it is! My vision is for people to have that opportunity to earn their own piece of the American Pie, be financially independent, leave their legacy, and build a better world for our future generations! Let it begin with you!

Starting out in anything can be scary, and that can be especially true when starting a business. Feeling afraid or insecure is a normal human emotion when doing anything new. If you could remember your feelings back to when you were a baby, you'd realize that you felt fear when you first learned to sit up, crawl, walk, or run. But you didn't let that stop you. You did it even though you were afraid. You trusted in yourself, keeping your faith and mindset focused on what you desired. You were determined. You knew if you were seeing others do it, you could do it too, and then you did.

That same positive mindset applies to what it takes to start a business and keep it going. The business profession you decide to pursue can be based on your skills or expertise. The habits you create will become your daily rituals. These rituals will become your compass on your road to success! I personally recommend you form rituals for both personal and business practices. Those habits will keep you fresh and performing at your optimal best. So, take some time to sit down and create these rituals to help you to operate successfully in your business and life.

Things to consider are time and money management. Watch your time and set limits on how much time to give yourself to get things done. Form a weekly exercise routine for optimal health. Create a daily habit of sitting alone with God, expressing gratefulness for all you have. Take time to meditate every morning on your dreams and how to accomplish them: feel them, see them, write them down! Make it your habit to write down and go over your next day's schedule the night before and first thing in the morning. Doing this will keep you organized and focused on completing your tasks on time. Set budgets and ensure good money practices are followed. Check and compare transactions on your bank and credit card accounts to prevent overdrafts, fraudulent or unauthorized charges, or missed payments due. Rituals are as easy to adopt as brushing your teeth. Rituals give peace, order, and confidence, which brings success.

I have been self-employed since I was eight years old. I wanted things. Things I soon realized required money. Coming from a family that had little money to give, I knew if I wanted money, I would have to get it on my own. That is when I created a habit of looking for ways to earn money, and services that people would pay me for. That is the day I stepped into my entrepreneurial shoes!

That summer, I grew pumpkins and sold them in the fall. I started cleaning houses and washing bikes and cars. I cut lawns, pulled weeds, raked leaves, and swept off sidewalks, driveways, garages, and porches. I made and sold things, including cookies and pet rocks. I made and sold Kool-Aid and lemonade. I babysat, sometimes for kids my own age! I even created a dog washing service. I created so much work for myself that I actually hired kids to work for me. Boy, was it fun! I didn't think about how I was going to do it; I just did it!

It didn't stop there. At age 15, I started painting homes. After that, I started a handyman service, which was influenced by my grandfather. The handyman service later led me back to the cleaning business. After marrying, my spouse and I started an electrical contracting business and then started building houses. This led me to design and decorate for not only myself but other builders as well. My first house design challenge was building a house around an old oak tree in order to save the tree. That house sold before it was even finished. My first copyright came from designing a house.

In my early twenties, I was faced with the prospect of having to solely operate our electrical company because my spouse wanted nothing more to do with it. Having faith and turning the company over to God, I took on the challenge. The company ended up growing so quickly it became necessary to hire more employees. We hit seven figures soon after. Praise God! The business became one of the state's leading electrical contractors, employing well over one hundred people at three locations and with over fifty vehicles on the road. It's amazing what God can do when we have faith, ask for His help, get committed, and take action.

I am so, grateful for all the creative talents and courage God has placed inside me as an entrepreneur! I'm so happy and grateful God blessed the fruits of my labor. Expressing gratitude every day will bring you more things to be grateful for. Just think of all the things and people that you are happy to have in your life. Express that appreciation for them in your heart daily. There is power in gratitude!

Expressing the things you're grateful for and writing them down in a notebook can become a ritual that you can do every night right before bed or at the start of your day. This is a highly recommended daily practice that will make you feel appreciation for what or who you have in your life! You can get started on it right now. Give it a shot! Ask yourself what ten things you're grateful for having in your life. Write them down. *The more you express gratitude the more things you will be blessed with in your life to be grateful for!*

"The starting point of all achievement is desire."
- Napoleon Hill

STARTING YOUR BUSINESS

Now that you've decided you want to earn a piece of the America Pie and go into business for yourself, you're probably asking yourself questions like: How do I start my own business? Is it going to be hard? Do I need money to get started? What are the legalities involved with running my own business? Can I work from my home or do I need to rent office space? How do I get my customers? Do I need a license? Will I need insurance? Is insurance expensive? How many hours a week will I need to work? How do I know if I'll be successful? Where do I begin?

Don't worry! I'm here to help you! You've made a smart choice in picking up this book because all the simple, easy-to-follow steps are all mapped out for you, making it easier than ever to start your business. I'll discuss getting started, operating your business, filing corporate papers, taxes, advertising, promotions, pricing your service, and so much more. I'll even give you a list of businesses that you could create for yourself that can all easily be operated right out of your home.

Follow along with me as I help you to get started living the American Dream of owning your own business here in the USA. You'll be living a life that's full of adventure and freedom. It's your birthright! Be that business owner you've always dreamt of being. It's your destiny to own a piece of the American Pie!

Your entrepreneurial spirit has come alive and is seeking more than the typical lifestyle of working for someone else. You knew it from the moment you set your intentions to get something better out of life. You've made a wise decision to go into business for yourself. Your intentions, followed by your actions, are why you are here. Your entrepreneurial spirit is beaming. Let your light shine! You're about to embark on a whole new adventure that will bring you great rewards.

"Entrepreneurs take the necessary risks, creating strategies to succeed."
- Tammy Mihalic

Entrepreneurs are not like most people! Being an entrepreneur is not for the faint of heart. You must have grit and determination. As an entrepreneur, you know what you want, and with integrity, you will do whatever it takes to get you to where it is you want to go. "No" or "I can't" are not part of your thinking or vocabulary.

Entrepreneurs take charge and are not afraid to lead their own lives or take risks. You know that starting and running your own business should not be taken lightly. You have backbone and know that being spineless will get you nowhere! You walk in confidence and know that what you want is attainable. You are dedicated to successfully planning and preparing for the launch and livelihood of your new business. You are committed to the hours that are necessary to get the business up and running. Enthusiastically, with a positive mindset, you stay passionate about pursuing your dream. You are determined and will not allow obstacles to deter you from reaching your goals or what you want out of life.

Entrepreneurs take the necessary risks and create strategies to succeed. As an entrepreneur, you know it takes more than just planning and creating your business strategy. It takes ACTION! You know that you can plan and prepare all day long, but unless you take action to get your business started, you'll never accomplish your dream. You know that some of the necessary actions that need to be taken are risky and sometimes downright scary, but you take them. You know and trust that you will reap the rewards for your bravery.

"It's your destiny to be rich and own a piece of the American Pie!"
- Tammy Mihalic

GOAL SETTING

In order to live a truly productive life, one must set goals. Goals should not be confused with your daily to-do lists, or task, that must get done. Goals are the things you find important, and want to accomplish in your life, and work best if they are written down and are given a deadline. A deadline will help you stay focused, but you must be determined, and take action steps every day to reach the goals by the deadline you have set. *Without having clearly written goals, we lose direction.* This principle behind writing your goals on paper is to inspire you to take action to achieve them. Looking at, and feeling the outcome of your goals completed should be a daily ritual. Goals should be set and implemented in both your personal life and your business operations.

What is the definition of goal setting to you? To me, it is identifying something that I want to accomplish for myself, in a measurable amount of time with a written action plan to actually do it! You can accomplish anything you see in your mind more quickly by writing it on paper. When you write your goals down and review them daily, not only do you connect to them, but you stay focused, and will see your vision more clearly and will accomplish them more quickly! Never take your eyes off of them! See them as done! *Keep your eyes on your goals like a programed address in your GPS!*

"A goal properly set is halfway reached."
- Zig Ziglar

As you know, it will be important to set goals on how you plan to grow your business and then commit to those goals. When you have goals that you are committed to, you perform better, are more organized, more efficient and you grow, also, be sure to reward yourself as you accomplish your goals. That reward will keep you motivated and operating at your optimal best. For example, you might set a goal to call ten new businesses every day until you have fifty new clients, and you give yourself four weeks to make it happen. Once you achieve the goal, you reward yourself with a weekend getaway to celebrate a job well done!

Feeling overwhelmed when creating goals? Relax! You may need a mental adjustment reminding you of your potential. Try breaking your goals down into smaller steps. It makes them much easier to accomplish and is less overwhelming. Then complete one step at a time without pressuring yourself.

Display your goals on your desk or on the wall in front of it. You can also jot them down on cards and keep them with you. Read them daily. Keep focused on accomplishing an action step toward your goals every day. Mark them off as they're completed, and reward yourself! Rewards will help to give you the incentive you may need to complete your goal. It'll be your way of thanking yourself for a job well done.

> *"Whatever the mind can conceive and believe, it can achieve."*
> **- Napoleon Hill**

Once you've accomplished your goal, write out the date it was achieved and display it as a reminder that you've successfully completed a goal. Displaying your achievements will give you the feeling of fulfillment and happiness. To feel fulfilled, we must have achievements in our lives. Displaying your achievements will remind you that you can do anything you put your mind to!

Stay excited about focusing on your goals. Keep motivated by reminding yourself of the end results, see them as done, and the reward you'll be giving yourself.

Tip: Write your goals out and visualize them as if they are already accomplished, with gratitude. Then read them every morning and evening at bed time. Get emotionally involved! Use the power of your thoughts to visualize the things you want as already having them. Be persistent. Take action steps daily toward completing your goals. If you have setbacks in achieving your goals, that's okay! It does happen. Simply be kind to yourself, don't judge it, and know that you can refocus and pick up where you left off tomorrow! Simply stay committed to completing your goals. Just keep putting one foot in front of the other. Then before you know it, you'll be accomplishing your goals in no time at all.

CREATE A SUCCESS PLAN

What does it take to create a successful business? First you must make a decision on what it is you want. Then you must plan out in detail how you plan to operate and manage your business. This is what is known as a business plan, and it is the foundation of your business. Your business plan needs to be well thought out because you'll be using it to help you run your business and keep organized. It will cover how your business is structured, how it is to be run, and how you plan to grow it. Business plans are also, useful when seeking funding or when bringing in investors or forming partnerships, because it will show them what steps you plan to take to make your business a profitable success. So, as you can see, it will be a very beneficial tool for your business!

If you fail to plan, you plan to fail! This old adage stands true to this day. So, make a plan and stick with it!

The business plan you create and execute will consist of at least four parts:

1. **A Financial Plan**: Tells you what steps to take to create a profitable business and meet your financial target.
2. **A Sales Plan**: Outlines how you plan to sell your business services to reach your target profit.

3. **A Marketing Plan**: Details who you're selling to and how you plan to reach that audience.
4. **An Operations Plan**: Covers how you will operate and manage your business and how you will plan for growth.

Plans are normally written and followed in one- to five-year increments. Plans can be changed, altered, or added to as needed. Flexibility is one of the perks of being in business for yourself, so, adjust your plans when necessary.

Starting out in business could be compared to planning a long road trip. Just like a road trip, you first need to know where it is you want to go. Which route do you want to take, and what type of transportation do you want to use to get there? What things do you need to pack, and what should you prepare for? What will be required for this trip? What can you do to ensure that it has every opportunity to be a successful, happy road trip? What kind of weather will you encounter that'll you'll need to be prepared for?

Once you have thought through all of these scenarios, you must put your plan into action by packing and loading the car. Now grab the mapped-out plan, put the key in the ignition, turn the engine on, put the car into drive, and begin your road trip!

A road trip can only be a road trip in a moving vehicle that's going places, not a parked car! These same principles will apply to starting out in business for yourself—create a plan and take action on that plan to get your business going!

Your business plan should entail; what kind of business you are in, how you will be operating that business, and its legal structure. It will describe what services or products you will be offering and the prices you will charge. It will also give a detailed description of your customers and what problems you solve for them. You will also write out your marketing strategies to create revenue for current and future sales of your company and any growth strategies you plan to implement. Your plan must also have deadlines. You must create a timeline as to when you will accomplish your plan within a one-, three-, and five-year span. Plus, don't forget to write your mission statement. It is important to state the reasons why you are in business and who you will serve. This will help people understand who you are and what role you will play in helping people.

For a free business plan sample, visit sba.gov or follow this link: https://www.sba.gov/sites/default/files/2017-09/Sample%20Business%20Plan%20-%20We%20Can%20Do%20It%20Consulting.doc

BASIC QUESTIONS TO ASK YOURSELF BEFORE GETTING STARTED:

- What kind of business do you want to start?
- Do you need additional skills or education for your business?
- Do you want to work from your home?
- How large do you want your company to become?
- How long to reach certain goals: two, three, five years?
- Do you want employees? (I highly recommend them.)
- How much money do you want to earn weekly, monthly, annually?
- How will your business help the people that you will serve in your community?
- What legacy do you wish to leave behind?
- Would you like to sell your business one day?

Imagine the final results first. Imagine what your business looks like once it has reached your success goals. Imagine the kind of customers you will be servicing and how you are making their lives better. Imagine the feeling you'll feel from having financial security and the freedom to buy those things that you have always dreamed of having. Imagine all of the people and charity's that you are helping. Imagine and feel the happiness from achieving success! Imagine leaving a legacy behind. This type of imagery process will help you to create the kind of business and lifestyle you want to experience. Set aside a good amount of time to do this and write down all of the creative things you come up with and keep them together in a folder. Go over them frequently to fine tune your desires.

After your own brainstorming session, **Create A Strategic Plan on Paper** to get you there, **Be Determined to Succeed and Take Action** with the plan!

Remember, just like the road trip, if you only plan it but never get into the car, put the key in the ignition, turn it on, and put it in drive, you'll never be able to take your trip. You must make preparations and take action. *Map out the steps to your business plan as thoroughly as possibly, be determined to make it happen, and then take action on your plan every day to get your business running!*

"Never begin the day until it is finished on paper."
- Jim Rohn

Here are some fun, basic things to know to help get you thinking outside the box prior to starting out in business. These are simply bits of inspiration to get you thinking about business.

- Know what really makes you happy and build your life around it. This keeps you feeling fulfilled.
- Know what type of business you want to have. This is where you start.
- Know the skills of the business you want to be in. This makes you qualified.
- Know the working hours needed for your business. This sets your schedule.
- Know how big you want your business to grow. It starts with a vision.
- Know how much money you want to earn. This will tell you how much you'll need to sell or how many hours you'll need to work.
- Know that it takes work. It's rarely handed to you!
- Know that if you don't do it, it won't get done! This brings completion.
- Know that it takes your commitment. This means don't stop believing.
- Know that running your own business requires taking action steps every day. Even a small step is a step. Keep your momentum moving forward, one step at a time! This keeps you feeling accomplished.
- Know that it's not easy. It's not hard. It just is! This means don't think about it, just do it!
- Know about how to budget your money. This keeps money in your pocket.
- Know how to stretch your dollar and get the most bang for your buck. This keeps you frugal.
- Know how to be your own teacher, boss, or drill sergeant. This builds motivating character!
- Know if you work hard for your money, your money will work hard for you.
- Know how to stand your ground. This protects you.
- Know how to say no. This stops regret.

- Know how to defend yourself diplomatically. This keeps the peace.
- Know how to ask for your money. This keeps your business profitable.
- Know how to pay your bills on time. This builds good credit.
- Know how to manage your time. This reduces stress.
- Know about exit strategies. This ensures your future.
- Know to ask quality questions. This keeps you highly informed.
- Know to ask for help. This will eliminate fear.
- Know that it takes time to grow a business. It's like being pregnant. You don't give birth the same day you conceive. You have to give your baby time to grow! Be patient with the process. This builds character.
- Know that even when you feel discouraged, motivate yourself and keep your eyes on the prize. This is so, you don't give up.
- Know success is in the knowing!

With so much knowledge available in our world, there really is no reason why we shouldn't be able to learn anything we need to know. There are many ways to learn and acquire knowledge, from buying a self-help book, which you've done here, to buying an online course or taking the long, lengthy, costly option of going back to school. I can tell you though, you don't need a certified education for every business. If you have the skills but simply need a license as proof of your expertise to operate your business, you can hire a certified licensee to represent your business and provide you with the license needed to operate your company. For a flat fee or a percentage of your gross sales, a qualifier will sign permits and oversee your work to ensure everything is to code. (See your local licensing board for qualifying requirement details.) There's also, the hands-on method, which is figuring it out on our own by trial and error. Hang out on the Internet or at the library for some fun research. You can also, ask to learn from someone who's already doing what you want to do. *If you need to know anything in life, find a way to learn it, and ask for help!*

Congratulations! You are an action taker! Stay excited because soon your business will be up and running and heading toward the finish line of financial success! Just imagine what that will feel like for you!

Remember, I can only guide you in the direction of success. Only you can guarantee it by applying your own effort. Your ambition will take you a long way if you do not quit. As you continue reading, you'll find tips to get organized and be efficient with your time. I'll discuss marketing, selling, and bidding your services to potential clients, along with simple techniques on communicating to ensure customer satisfaction, plus ways to take care of yourself, and so, much more.

"Life takes on meaning when you become motivated, set goals, and charge after them in an unstoppable manner."
- Les Brown

What are your goals? What will your business plan look like?

_____

_____

_____

_____

_____

_____

_____

_____

_____

_____

_____

_____

_____

_____

_____

_____

_____

_____

_____

_____

_____

_____

_____

_____

_____

_____

_____

_____

3

MAKING YOUR BUSINESS LEGAL

I n this chapter, I'll lay out the appropriate guidelines for starting your business and brief you on the terminology and the process of creating your new business. Making your business legal means complying with all federal, state, and local government regulations that are necessary for operating and paying taxes on your business in the state where it's governed or formed.

When forming any new business, you must decide if you will be operating your business from your home or from a separate building location. You then must see if your location is zoned for your business type and what requirements you must follow. Your business type will be labeled with a code that determines where you can operate your business and any associated fees. Many businesses can and do operate right out of their primary residence. Your jurisdiction's zoning department will have that information and help you decide.

Once your location is decided upon, you must register your business name and legal entity with your Secretary of State (SOS). (Note: Sole proprietors are not required to file with the SOS.) You can file the paperwork on your own or contact a certified public account

(CPA) or a tax attorney for help. They both will know the tax laws and will be able to help determine which type of business entity to form. Certified professionals will get you through all the red tape, save you lots of valuable time, and give you peace of mind knowing your business is set up properly.

There are also, self-help websites like www.Legalzoom.com that are very easy to use. They ask you a list of questions and have you fill out a questionnaire. After that is completed, they help set up your business entity for a fee. They also, offer attorneys for hire and accounting advice. Ask for cost up-front before committing to their services. From my personal experience, their services were useful.

CHOOSING AND REGISTERING YOUR BUSINESS NAME

Well, first, you must decide what type of business you'll be creating. This will help to determine your company's name and what business structure to use. All businesses will follow the same procedure when registering their business name.

What should you name your business? Depending on your business type, you can actually use your personal name for your business name while adding your service after it. You then could operate your business as a sole proprietor. Many people start out in business this way. So, if your name was Sally Goldstein, and you wanted to start a house-sitting service, your business would be called Sally Goldstein, followed by what work you are providing, for example, house sitting service. Then when you were ready to advertise your business or make your business cards, your name would appear something like this: *House Sitting by Sally Goldstein*, or *Sally Goldstein: House Sitting Service*. This tells what service you offer and who is offering it. Clients would then write a check personally to Sally Goldstein. Using your name as your business name is much simpler when you're first starting out and, for tax purposes, and will only require using your social security number to operate.

Now, if you want to use a business name other than your name, you would simply apply for what's known as a "fictitious name," also, known as "doing business as" or DBA. Then it might look something like this: *Sally Goldstein, DBA Golden Touch House Sitting*. Your clients would then pay your business name, *Golden Touch House Sitting*, instead of you personally.

If you do decide you want to call your business something other than your own name, you'll need to research that name to make sure no one is already using it for a business in your community. To see if someone is using that name, start your search by using several search engines, such as Google, Bing, Yahoo, Baidu, and DuckDuckGo. Search www.yellowpages.com, social media, Yelp, and Trademark.com. Search domain names to see if your desired name is available. If your domain name is available, you should purchase that name immediately! This will secure your name for your website once you are ready to create one.

Once you've researched your potential name online, your next step is to go to your local county clerk's office. There, you can review the local business name registry to determine if anyone within your county is using the name you want to use. If it's available, then your next step is to register that name with your local county officials. After that, you will need to register the name with the Secretary of States' office, where they'll take on the task of doing your business name search on a state level. There will be a processing fee for this service. Once you receive documentation that your name is clear, you can file for your state registration, declaring the name is yours to use in the state where you live. Many of these services are available online through your city's .gov website.

WHAT IS A FICTITIOUS NAME?

A fictitious name is a made-up name under which you perform business in your state, other than your legal birth name. Your business name should be simple, yet unique, easy to pronounce, but memorable. Say it out loud to see if it has a nice ring to it. Ask friends and family what they think about the name. Does it match your business or convey your line of work? How does it compare to other names of companies in your industry?

After you have picked your name, your next step is to legally file for a fictitious name. It's a fairly easy process and should cost under a hundred dollars. It is required if you will be doing business under a name other than your own name. Filing for a fictitious business name establishes you as a community business.

You will be required to run an ad in your local newspaper to announce your fictitious name, also, known as "Doing Business As" (DBA). This is standard practice and dates back to the colonial era. It allows the local community in which you live to know that you have formed a business.

You will need the fictitious business name document to open up your business bank account and credit accounts with your suppliers. Without it, you have no real legal standing for operating your business with that name. This will not apply if you're a sole proprietor using your own name.

APPLYING FOR A BUSINESS LICENSE

Once your ownership and your name are registered, you're ready to receive a business license. In some places, you will only be required to file for a business tax certificate. The legal criteria for licensing will vary depending on the state, county, or city you live in. You will need to check with your local county clerk's office for the information to verify their license requirements.

As the owner of a business, you are required to comply with all federal, state, and local regulations. Unless you are a sole proprietor, you must register your business in order to file tax documents. Without the proper license and registration, you are not considered a legitimate business, and therefore you are not entitled to any federal or state tax break opportunities.

Tax breaks are the number one reason why a person should go into business for themselves. The tax write-offs for your business is the "secret" of the rich! Without tax breaks, it's harder for an individual to get ahead financially. Our government allows these tax breaks and deductions so, that your business can grow and profit. So, be sure to take advantage of these tax breaks that you are legally entitled to.

Registering your business is where many businesses fall short. It separates the professionals from the work-for-cash operations. If a lawsuit were to be filed against you and it was discovered that you didn't have a license to operate your business, you could be hit with fines.

Normally, when operating a business under your own name as opposed to a fictitious one, you do not need to get a license. Procedures do vary by state. I recommend contacting your Secretary of State to determine all the requirements for your particular business.

Before choosing your entity, consider your business, its liability, and your personal assets at risk. How you register your business will determine how you will file your income taxes and which tax form you will be required to use. The common ways to form your business are to register as a sole-proprietorship, a corporation, or as a partnership if you're going into business with another person. If you have decided to register as a limited liability company (LLC), you will need to know your state's statutes because every state has different requirements and fees for an LLC.

You will also, need to decide your "tax year." A tax year is your annual accounting period, which is the time frame you document and report your business's income and expenses. The tax years to choose from are:

- **A Calendar year** - Twelve consecutive months starting on January 1st and ending December 31st.
- **A Fiscal year** - Twelve consecutive months ending in the last month of the twelfth month from when it began. If you began in July, your fiscal year would end the following year in June. A fiscal tax year varies from 52 to 53 weeks and does not have to end on the last day of a month, but could end a week or two before.

Listed below are the common types of corporate filing formats that are available for you to choose from, plus a few pros and cons and how each type is taxed. This will give you a better understanding of which corporate filing is best suited for your business when forming your new company. Most of this can be done online.

SOLE PROPRIETORSHIPS

As a sole proprietor, you are not required to register or file your name with the government to form your business. However, you may still need business permits and licenses to operate lawfully. If you go into business for yourself and you're the sole owner, then you're considered to be a sole proprietor. As a sole proprietor, it is required that the legal name of your business be your own name. In a sole proprietorship, the federal and state income tax laws view you and your business as one.

If you would rather not have your business name be your own name, you can choose to operate the business under another name, known as a "fictitious business name" or "doing business as" (also, known as DBA). It would look like the sample I talked about at the beginning of this chapter in the section entitled Choosing and Registering Your Business Name.

Example: Sally Goldstein, DBA Golden Touch House Sitting. *Note: In most states, you will be required to file an application for your DBA.

As a sole proprietorship, it's a good idea to have two bank accounts: one business and one personal. This will help you to keep your business expenses separate from your personal expenses. It will help you monitor, track, and record your business expenses and will make it easier to accurately report your business income or losses at the end of the year on your tax returns. Most banks will allow you to open an account for your sole proprietorship business using only your social security number, also make sure to get a credit card that is for business use only. Without it, you will not be able to deduct any interest or fees billed.

SOLE PROPRIETORSHIPS: PROS

- Require the least amount of money, time, and effort to create.
- Have tax advantages.
- Easy record keeping.
- You are your own boss and can operate with a spouse.
- Not required to file annual reports or quarterly filings.
- Less governmental control.
- You can easily convert your sole proprietorship into another type of business entity, such as a partnership, LLC or corporation.

SOLE PROPRIETORSHIPS: CONS

- You're completely responsible for the business.
- You're the only one doing the work.
- May be difficult getting traditional financing.
- You're personally liable for business claims or lawsuits.
- You're personally liable for all company financial obligations should the company fail.
- What you own is at stake.

HOW ARE SOLE PROPRIETORS TAXED?

As a sole proprietor, you will be required to file a Schedule C, a Schedule SE, and Form 1040 with the IRS. Schedule C is used to determine your net income by calculating your business's income and expenses. That net income will be filed on your personal income tax returns; the business itself is not taxed. This is what is known as pass-through taxation, where your business profits are passed through the business and taxed on your personal income tax return (Form 1040). Any losses that you suffer would be subtracted from your annual income tax bill. Your business and personal taxes will be calculated at the same rate because your business earnings are considered your personal earnings as a sole proprietor.

Once your business is profitable, you will be required to pay the taxes on a monthly or quarterly basis. As a sole proprietor, you will also, make your own contribution to Social Security and Medicare, and that will be done on the Schedule SE form.

LIMITED LIABILITY COMPANY (LLC)

A limited liability company, better known as an LLC, is created under the statutes of the state where it is formed. LLC owners are called members. What's unique about an LLC in most states is its ownership. There does not have to be a limited number of members. Members can be individuals, corporations, other LLCs, or a foreign entity, which will require special rules to join. You can also file as only one owner.

When an LLC has two or more members, it is considered a partnership, and each owner will be required to file their taxes separately. They can also choose to be treated as a corporation by filing Form 8832, known as the "Entity Classification Election." This form tells how the LLC will be classified, such as a partnership, a corporation, or a foreign entity, and will state how the members of the LLC will be taxed. All members must sign a consent form confirming this action. You can also, elect to file as an S Corp by filing Form 2553, bypassing Form 8832 entirely. Qualifications and stipulations will apply. See: S Corp section in this chapter.

An LLC offers the same protection as a corporation, provided there is an operating agreement. This agreement should define the assignability of interest, management, and distribution of profit and losses.

LLC: PROS

- It's easy to form and maintain.
- Personal assets are not at risk if the business goes into debt or declares bankruptcy.
- The LLC is the only one responsible for its debt.
- The LLC does not pay income tax on the business, but rather each member of the LLC pays taxes on their share of profits or would deduct their share of the losses against their personal income when filing their personal tax return.
- Profits or losses are divided among the owners equally or as stated in the operating agreement and are filed on the members' personal income tax returns. (An operating agreement defines how the profits and losses will be split among the members and how major business decisions will be made.)
- There are no restrictions on the number of foreign shareholders in the U.S.
- One person can be the sole member in most states.
- A very unique advantage of the LLC is that it can elect to be taxed as an S Corporation or even a C Corporation if it chooses.

- Member certificates, instead of stock, are issued for the percentage of ownership owned. A laws book should be maintained for the issuance of these member certificates.

LLC: CONS

- Not all businesses can operate as an LLC, and it varies from state to state.
- Traditional loans aren't always easy to get.
- More tax forms are required and are filed annually.
- Annual meetings are required. All meeting minutes must be registered and kept in a minute/by laws book.
- Must file annual reports, which are required by most states and require a fee to stay current and update members involved.
- You must file for a Federal Identification Number (EIN) this also will be required to open your bank account.

HOW ARE LLCS TAXED?

An LLC will have flexibility in how it is taxed. This will depend on how many members it has and the tax treatment applied. An LLC can be taxed as a corporation, an S-Corp, a partnership, or a sole proprietorship. An LLC with two or more members is automatically taxed as a partnership unless they file IRS Form 8832 to elect to be treated as a corporation. An LLC with only one owner will be taxed as a sole proprietorship unless the company files Form 8832 with the IRS requesting a different tax application. As always, speak to an accountant to help with this decision.

CORPORATIONS (C CORPORATION, C CORP)

A Corporation, also known as a C Corp, is normally formed for larger companies with multiple employees. The corporation is structured as an independent legal entity that is owned by the shareholders but guided by a board of directors who then elect officers such as a president, vice president, executive director, secretary, and treasurer, who conduct the day-to-day affairs of the business.

Corporations are liable for the obligations and debts the business incurs, not the shareholders, and must follow standard protocols of keeping good records and are required to hold, document, and record minutes of meetings held with the shareholders and the board of directors. All corporate minutes should be registered and kept in a minute/by laws book. Issuance of stock certificates should also, be recorded in the same fashion. The corporation is responsible for paying appropriate taxes, filing required documents with the Secretary of State, and preparing annual reports.

A corporation is formed under the laws of the state in which it is registered. To form a corporation, you'll need to establish your business name and register your company name with your state government. If you choose to operate under a different name other than the officially registered name, you'll be required to file an application for your fictitious name (DBA). Laws vary from state to state. It would look something like this: **Sally's Group, Inc. DBA Golden Touch House Sitting.** However, your business would operate under the name Golden Touch House Sitting.

Corporations must also include a corporate designation such as Corporation (Corp.), Incorporated (Inc.), or Limited (Ltd.) at the end of their business name. Certain documents must be filed to register your corporation, typically known as articles of incorporation, which includes the basic required information about your company. This is then filed with your state's Secretary of State office. Corporations will be required to establish directors and issue stock certificates to the initial shareholders during the registration process.

Contact the business registration office for your specific filing requirements in the state where you are forming your business. You must obtain business licenses and permits once your business is registered. Regulations do vary by industry, state, and local city laws. Contact your local county clerk and licensing department to find a listing of federal, state, and local requirements for the permits, licenses, and registrations that you'll need to run a business.

Articles of Incorporation provide the state with the information about your business, which will also be public record for anyone to see. The articles include:

- Company name: and its identity such as Incorporated, Corporation, or Company, which can be abbreviated.
- Business purpose: which explains your business.
- Legal address of the business.
- Registered agent: the one who will receive tax and legal info for the corporation, which will require a physical address, not a PO Box. Often this address is that of an attorney.
- The Incorporator: the representative of the corporation filing the Articles, requiring their name, address, and signature.
- Number of authorized shares of stock: representing ownership.
- Share par value of the stock.
- Preferred shares or common shares: defines the dividend rate and when distributions are made.
- Directors: those overseeing the corporation's affairs and who are responsible for making important corporate decisions.

- Officers: such as the president, vice president, executive director, secretary, and treasurer, those who operate the day-to-day affairs of the company.

CORPORATION (C CORP): PROS

- Is liable for the business debts or losses, not the shareholders.
- The shareholders' personal assets are protected.
- Can sell stock to generate investment capital. Stock must be registered and kept in a laws book.
- Corporations file their taxes separately from the shareowners.
- Corporation owners only pay taxes on corporate profits paid to them in the form of salaries and/or in dividends.
- Offers competitive benefits for employees and offers them the potential for partial ownership of the corporation through stock options.

CORPORATION (C CORP): CONS

- Costly, requires more paperwork, is time-consuming to start and operate.
- Double taxation. Income is taxed when the company makes a profit, and the shareholders pay taxes on the income when it is distributed to them as dividends.
- Regulations applied to corporations by federal, state, and in some cases, local agencies, require additional paperwork and recordkeeping.
- Must file for a Federal Identification Number (EIN) this will be needed to open up your bank account.

HOW ARE CORPORATIONS TAXED?

Corporations and the owners are separate legal entities. A corporation must file a corporate tax return on Form 1120 and pay income taxes on its profits, unlike sole-proprietorships, partnerships, S corporations, or an LLC. With these entities, the profits or losses are passed through to the business owners and reported on their personal tax returns. Employees of the corporation who are also corporate owners will pay individual income tax on their salaries or bonuses received. Salaries and bonuses paid to employees are deductible expenses for the corporation. However, when dividends are distributed to the owners, they must report it as personal income and pay taxes on the amount. Dividends are not a deductible expense, and the corporation must pay taxes on the profits used to pay the dividends. Thus the profits used to pay the dividends are ultimately taxed twice, once by the corporation and again by the shareholder. Corporations are required to register and file a tax return with the IRS, as well as state and local revenue agencies.

SUBCHAPTER CORPORATION (S CORPORATION, S CORP)

A Subchapter Corporation, also known as an S Corp, is one of the more popular ways to file, but it must file as a corporation first before electing to file as an S Corporation. After the company is considered a legal corporation, all shareholders must sign and file Form 2553, electing the corporation to become an S Corporation. The IRS has stipulations and qualifications that must be met in order to become an S Corp. To qualify the corporation must first acquire assets, operate as a business or have shareholders. Once either one of these are met, you will only have two and a half months to file this election for it to be valid for that year. If you miss that deadline, your business will remain a C Corporation for the remainder of that year and will become an S Corp the following year, unless a late filing election is requested with reasonable cause for not filing form 2553 on time. Once certified, the S Corp taxes would then be filed on Form 1120S. The income and deductions allocated to each shareholder will then be reported on a Schedule K-1 form.

Once your business is registered, you must obtain licenses and permits based on your state's requirements to operate your business as an S Corp. What makes the S Corp different from a traditional corporation (C Corp) is that profits and losses are passed through to the shareholder's personal tax return. These profits cannot come until each owner who also works as an employee earns a reasonable compensation. (e.g., salary). An S Corp is not a legal entity, but is actually a tax election that is created through the IRS— the IRS is only responsible for taxation, not the formation of the business entity, which is in the domain of the Secretary of State.

S CORPORATION: PROS

- Tax savings and advantages.
- Pass-through taxation.
- Avoids double taxation.
- Limited liability; your personal assets are protected.
- Owner can receive salary and dividend payments.
- Shareholders do not pay self-employment tax on their share of the business's profits.

S CORPORATION: CONS

- Stricter qualification requirements.
- Requires scheduled director and shareholder meetings.
- Limited to one class of stock.
- Corporate officer compensation requirements. A corporate officer must receive reasonable compensation. The IRS takes notice of shareholder red flags like low salary/high distribution combinations and may reclassify your distributions as wages.
- Your Corp EIN may or may not pass through to your S Corp and you may be required to file for a new one. Visit, www.IRS.gov - for further details.

HOW ARE S CORPORATIONS TAXED?

An S corporation is not generally taxed on its income but rather makes the shareholder responsible for paying the tax by passing its profits or losses of the corporation to the individual shareholders. However, certain situations could require the S Corp to pay tax on built-in capital gains. You will also, need to register with the IRS, through state and local revenue agencies, and obtain a tax ID number. Not all states tax S Corps. In most states, the tax regulations are similar to the federal government, and the shareholders are taxed accordingly.

PARTNERSHIPS

A Partnership is a business arrangement formed anytime two or more people or entities agree to go into business together, sharing equally (or as defined in the partnership agreement) in all assets, property, labor, skills, profits, and financial and legal liabilities of the partnership. Partners are seen as the entities responsible for running or managing the day-to-day business. It is a good idea to write up a partnership agreement and formalize the details of a partnership that specifies each partner's rights, responsibilities, and the share of the profits and losses.

Once partners are engaged in a business, each partner is personally liable for the actions of that business, including the obligations of the other partners. With a partnership, there are no shields against personal liability.

If liability protection is important to you, consider a different business structure.

PARTNERSHIPS: PROS

- Partnerships can be structured however the partners want it.
- Partners each bring their own skills, expertise, and experience to the business.
- Partners share in the work of building the business.
- Inexpensive to start.
- Operates by a partnership agreement.
- If a partner drops out of a partnership composed of two or more partners, or a new partner joins, depending on the partnership agreement, it will not have to dissolve. A partnership can also swap out one partner with another without dissolving the partnership. Many consulting and accounting firms are set up as partnerships. Partners come and go without the partnerships having to dissolve.

PARTNERSHIPS: CONS

- Offers no asset protection.
- No shields against personal liability. Partners are liable for partners' actions in the business. This is true in all partnerships. If a business were to suffer a loss due to one partner, all partners would suffer the consequences. In the form of a partnership known as a limited partnership, only the general partners operate the business. The limited partners participate in the ownership of the partnership, but the limited partners do not have the legal right to make business decisions.
- If a partner drops out of the partnership and there are only two partners, the partnership must dissolve.
- Must file for a Federal Identification Number (EIN) this will also be needed to open up your bank account.
- If disputes were to arise, dissolving a partnership can be a legal nightmare, especially if the partnership agreement fails to describe rules for dissolving the partnership.

HOW ARE PARTNERSHIPS TAXED?

With a partnership, the business does not pay federal income tax. Instead, the income and deductions flow through to each partner like a sole proprietor using the pass-through system, and each partner is issued a Schedule K-1 form. The partners are then responsible for reporting each of their shares from the partnership on their personal income tax returns. The partnership itself would be required to file Form 1065, U.S. Return of Partnership Income.

I'll be the first to tell you, I am not a tax expert, nor do I claim to be one! That is why I pay good money to be protected! I hire a Certified

Public Accountant (CPA). It only makes good business sense. In my opinion, once your business is well established, you'll need a CPA, as well as an in-house accountant to run your everyday books and payroll.

If your in-house accountant is not well-qualified, you could miss out on a lot of valuable tax deductions that you're entitled to. Of course, qualifications vary from accountant to accountant. One reason for having a CPA in addition to an in-house accountant is to have a second set of eyes besides your own watching over your business's (MONEY). This helps to curtail embezzlement, saving you money in the long run!

For more information about corporate tax laws and required business regulations, visit: www.IRS.gov.

WHAT IS AN EIN?

An employer identification number (EIN) is your federal tax ID, also known as a Federal Tax Identification Number (FEIN). It's used to identify a business entity for tax purposes. It's like a Social Security number for a business. In general, you will need an EIN to operate your business. (LLC, C Corp, S Corp, Partnership)

If you are a sole proprietorship without employees, you can use your own Social Security number as your business identifier. However, if you hire employees, you'll be required to apply for an EIN. You may also need one when conducting business with a bank or lender as a sole proprietor.

If you are a single-member LLC, you are required to apply for an EIN even if you do not hire employees in most states. This is so that the IRS can identify your business entity for tax filing purposes. You would still be required to give your Social Security number to another business requesting your tax ID on Form W-9, instead of your EIN, if they hired you. A multi-member LLC would be required to provide their EIN, if requested, on Form W-9, while on their individual personal tax return, Form 1040, Schedule C, the EIN would be included where indicated, even if it's not used for payroll tax purposes.

Here is the IRS link to get your free FEIN once you're ready: https://sa.www4.irs.gov/modiein/individual/index.jsp

OPENING YOUR BANKING ACCOUNT

Opening up a business banking account should be a fairly simple process, and makes your business look legitimate in the eyes of the IRS, even as a sole proprietor. You will want to keep your personal bank account, separated from your business bank account. Having separate bank accounts makes it easier to track company expenses and income for tax purposes.

Normally, using your Social Security number is all that is required to open a business bank account when you are a sole proprietor, even if operating under a fictitious name. However, some banks will require you to obtain a FEIN. This will depend on your banking institution.

In order to open up a business bank account as an LLC, Corporation, S Corp, or Partnership, you'll be required to obtain a FEIN, and must bring all paperwork that shows proof of your business name, including your articles of incorporation, which is established on your state's Secretary of State website.

You might want to interview several banks to determine which bank will work best for your business banking needs. Make sure to ask about monthly fees, regulations, and minimum balance requirements. Each bank's policies for opening up a business account will vary. See your bank for requirement details.

METHODS OF GETTING PAID

Getting paid on time is an important part of your business. The type of business you have, and state regulations, will determine how you will collect your funds. Typically, by law, a customer has 30 days from the time of billing to pay their bill. If the bill is paid after the due date you can charge a finance charge on that balance. You have the option to charge a flat rate that cannot exceed the balance owed, or a monthly finance fee on the overdue amount. Typically, companies will charge a 1 to 1.5% monthly late fee, which is 12 to 18% annually on the balance owed. Late fees are normally implemented on those customers who refuse to pay in a timely manner after passing the 30-day due date. Each situation should be handled as you see fit. I recommend your company policy state in clear terms that you are to be paid on the day you complete the job. If your business is dealing with larger jobs, you may need to break your work and payments into draws, based on the percent of completion. For example, you can bill for 50 percent of the job once half has been completed. Once paid, you'd complete the remaining 50 percent of the job and then bill and collect the balance when you're done. Always bill and collect on time. Don't wait for your money! You'll find that most customers have no problem paying you at the time service is rendered. All you have to do is ask. I recommend you make that your company policy. You'll thank me for it later.

There are many ways to get paid for your services; consider these options to see which work best for you. Please note that these installed apps and pay sources require your credit card and bank information before they can be used.

- **Cash** is the simplest and most common way of receiving payment. When receiving cash, remember to document who paid you with cash and how much, also it's very important to write down the date you received payment and get a signature. You would never want to mistakenly bill a customer twice or notify them that they are late on their payment because you forgot to record their cash payment.
- **Checks** are a form of payment that will require a banking institution. If you decide to accept checks, make sure you have a policy in place to pass on to the customer any bank fees that the bank will charge you for, like insufficient funds or returned checks. Clearly state this in the contract between you and your customer and have them initial the description of the fee policy. Usually, you will charge the customer for the bank fees and your company fees. For example, if the bank charges you $29 for a returned check charge, you will pass that fee on to them along with your own company's fee of $25 or whatever fee you decide. You would then be able to charge the customer $54 ($29 bank fee + $25 your fee). This additional fee is entirely up to you, but I recommend it because it will keep it from happening, and if it does, you will be paid to deal with it.
- **Money orders**: Cashier checks, certified checks, and wire transfers are other forms of payment.
- **Credit Cards** will require you to set up what is known as a merchant account. This will be done through your banking

institution or other payment companies. However, they are not free. Merchant accounts come with fees and will vary per bank. **See your banking institution for fee structures**. Make sure you understand how the entire credit card process works and who to contact if a problem or a question arises. Card fees vary per credit card company. MasterCard and Visa offer a lower fee compared to companies like Discover or American Express, which usually have higher fees. See your bank for those fees.

- **PayPal** is another source for receiving payment. According to PayPal, there are no fees to use PayPal to purchase goods or services. However, if you receive money for goods or services (such as from selling services to a client), there is a fee for each transaction. This fee can be passed on to the customer if you state in your policy that you charge an additional fee for using credit cards or PayPal.

- **Apps** are another way to receive payment. Today, with practically everyone owning a smartphone, and using the internet, you can use an app like Venmo, or PayPal, assuming your customer also uses them. You then transfer the money from that account to your bank.

- **Google Pay,** also known as G Pay, is another secure way to receive payment. This is an app to install on your phone and can be used with any smartphone. Many online stores are now using Google Pay as a way of receiving payment from customers.

- **Apple Pay** works on all your Apple devices. This is a preinstalled app in your Wallet on your Apple devices. You must configure Apple Pay to a credit card and bank account before using Apple Pay to receive payments. Payments can be sent and received in Messenger.

"Never spend your money before you have earned it."
- Thomas Jefferson

What business names and structure are you considering?

_____

_____

_____

_____

_____

_____

_____

_____

_____

_____

_____

_____

_____

_____

_____

_____

_____

_____

_____

_____

_____

_____

_____

_____

_____

_____

_____

_____

_____

_____

4

TAXES

Taxes! What are they, and why do we have them? Taxes are a mandatory financial charge imposed upon a business or individual by a government organization to fund various public, common, and agreed on national needs and government functions. Failure to pay is punishable by law.

As a business owner, you will be the one responsible for filing the reports and paying the taxes for your company. The forms you file and how your taxes are paid are determined by your business structure. (Corp, S-Corp, LLC, SP). The United States Congress passes the laws governing federal taxation, and the Internal Revenue Code set by the Internal Revenue Service (IRS) establishes the regulations that govern the filing of the returns. The IRS provides a service to file tax returns electronically as a convenience to taxpayers. State and local governments, which impose income and sales taxes, set the filing requirements for payment of those taxes. For a fee, you can hire a CPA to help you determine your taxable income, the amount of tax owed, and which forms to file.

For more details on filing and paying your business taxes, contact the IRS at: https://www.irs.gov/businesses/small-businesses-self-employed/filing-and-paying-your-business-taxes

As a business, you'll have expenses to offset your income, so, stay organized and keep good records and save all of your receipts. The ability to reduce your taxable income by deducting expenses is one of the very reasons you want to be self-employed and own your own business. Many of your expenditures are only allowed to be deducted if you own a business. That is the secret of the rich and how they keep more money in their pocket! Tax deductions are how you will get ahead too! Only as a business can you write off the many expenses you'll have that you could never write off as an employee.

If you have decided to operate your business from your home, which I highly recommend, you'll be allowed to deduct a specific portion of your home expenses on your taxes as well. That is, if your home office space qualifies! In order to qualify for this home-based deduction, you must pass the "exclusive use test" (see: www.IRS.gov Publication 587); that is, you must be using the deductible space of your home exclusively and regularly for business only. This area is not to be used for any other purpose.

Your office is the place where you perform all your administrative functions for your business and is the place where you meet with your clients. Home office deductions that may apply include your office equipment such as your copier, printer, computer, fax machine, phone landline, cell phone and Internet services, office supplies, equipment, furniture, decorations, licenses, security system, a portion of property tax, liability and bonding insurance, utilities, mortgage interest, mortgage insurance, HOA fees, janitorial services, remodeling, maintenance and repairs, etc. See your accountant or the

IRS.gov website for a more detailed list of all the items that may qualify.

Business Deductions

In order for your business to be eligible to deduct expenses, you must make a profit. Money spent in pursuit of earning a profit is deductible. You must show a profit in any two years of the first five-year period in business. So, if you ran a pop-up store and traveled all over your state, your travel expenses (hotel, meals, gas, etc.) and equipment (tent, tables, signs, etc.) would be deductible provided you earned a profit because those expenses came about while you were in pursuit of earning a profit.

Common Business Deductions

- **Accounting** - Hiring an accountant for your business is a fully deductible expense.
- **Advertising** - Any ad placed in newspapers, magazines, flyers, mail inserts, business cards, brochures, signs, magnetic car signs, stickers, websites, social media, fundraisers, or sponsorships is fully deductible.
- **Automobile Expenses** - You can deduct a percentage of your car expenses or only your miles based on the IRS's standard mileage rate. You cannot do both. Car expenses include: license, registration fees, insurance, maintenance, repairs, tires, tolls, parking, and fuel. You must keep all receipts and maintain good records of all of these expenses. I recommend keeping a labeled monthly envelope in your car to keep such receipts and documentation. This will really help you stay organized and on

top of your record keeping. Recording and documenting expenses as you go is much easier than going back and trying to figure it all out at the end of the month. Take the time and record as you go. Don't forget to add any commuting miles for travel to meet a client, to perform a job outside the home, to purchase business supplies, to conduct research, or to do any other kind of activity for your business. Travel expenses are deductible to the extent that the travel is for a business purpose.

- **Cell Phone Cost and Service Plan** - The cost of your cell phone and its usage for business can be fully deductible.
- **Charity or Donations** - Any money, equipment, or supplies given to charity is a deductible expense. The IRS sets rules for the amount that can be deducted. Limitations are set on the number of charitable contributions that can be deducted each tax year.
- **Clothing or Uniform** - Work clothes that can double as regular wear are not deductible. Clothing or uniforms that are mandatory for the workplace and unsuitable for everyday wear are deductible.
- **Computer Software** - depending on your business usage, you can choose to expense the cost in the year you acquire it or depreciate it over a given number of years according to depreciation rules set by the IRS.
- **Equipment for Cleaning** - Equipment such as a vacuum, carpet cleaners, mops, brooms, dustpans, toilet brush, etc., are deductible.
- **Equipment for Office** - Desks, computers, printers, scanners, fax machines, chairs, lamps, etc., may qualify for a full deduction of its expense, or you may consider them as assets and have to depreciate their use based on IRS guidelines.

- **Health Insurance** - As a self-employed business owner, a percentage of your entire premium is deductible provided you earn a profit.
- **Home Office Space** - Home office deductions can only qualify if you pass the IRS exclusive use test. If your home is your "principal" place of business and you are using your home office space "exclusively and regularly" to operate your business with the intention of earning a profit, the IRS will allow you to write off expenses for rent, mortgage, utilities, real estate taxes, insurance, repairs, and maintenance. The home office deductions cannot exceed the business's gross income and must be used exclusively for business. Your dining room table where you have family dinners would not qualify because you eat there.

There are two ways to determine your deductions. One way is the actual expense method. It requires you to save receipts and record all home expenses. You then must determine the percentage of office space you are occupying compared to the square footage of your home by dividing the square footage of your office by the square footage of your house. That number is the percentage you're allowed to deduct from your overall home expense as an indirect expense. You can also deduct direct expenses relating to the office space, such as painting, adding new flooring, cabinets, electrical, lighting, A/C, or repairs. This method requires a bit of time to figure out, and you may need help from your accountant. To help you figure out which expenses can be deducted, use Tax Form 8829.

Alternatively, there is the simple method. Generally, you're allowed an office space up to 300 square feet, and the IRS allows you a deduction of five dollars per square foot. That's a whopping $1500 you can deduct from your taxes for running your business from your home. Just imagine the savings! These home deductions rules can apply to your garage, barn, shed, or any freestanding structure, providing they meet the "exclusive and regular use" requirements. You can read more about it at www.IRS.gov. Simply put "home office tax deductions" in the search box to read a more in-depth description of all the requirements. You may also consult your accountant for exact details.

- **Internet Expenses** - All business-related Internet expenses, such as the cost to create or maintain a web page or Internet usage, are fully deductible. (BE CAREFUL - if the same Internet connection could be used for personal usage or by other members of the family, then only part of the cost is deductible based on the percent of the time it is used for business.)
- **Legal Fees** - Attorney fees pertaining to the business are fully deductible.
- **Licenses and Registration Fees** - All licenses and registration fees related to your business are fully deductible.
- **Meals with a Client for Lunch** - Taking a client to lunch is a standard practice for a business; 50 percent of the meal is deductible. You must provide documentation such as who attended and what business was discussed.
- **Office Supplies** - Deduct supplies such as pens, paper, business cards, brochures, envelopes, paper clips, phone, trash can, calendars, schedule book, Thank You cards, and whatever else you may need to operate, maintain, and organize your business.
- **Retirement Plan** - As a self-employed business owner, it's smart to put money into a tax-deferred retirement plan, such as an IRA, so, that you can receive a tax deduction on your contribution.
- **Subscriptions** - Newspapers, magazines, or journals that are business-related are fully deductible.

- **Supplies for Customer** - Any supplies you supply for your customers are fully deductible. These items will vary by business type.
- **Telephone Expenses for a Second Line** - A line dedicated for business is fully deductible. The same is true for cell phones.
- **Travel Expenses** - If you attend a conference for business purposes or travel to meet a client, even if in Spain, you can deduct your transportation costs such as plane tickets, bus fare, taxes, airport parking, car rental, lodging, meals, and even tips.

Tax Thoughts

If you have any tax questions or concerns, it's always best to consult a tax professional or the IRS. An accountant (CPA) knows the law and will help you to minimize your tax bill legally. Not all accountants are the same, so, shop around and find the best accountant that you feel will represent your business and keep you from overpaying your taxes. When it comes to the IRS and taxes, you never want to bend the rules. You should always make sure you're taking all the deductions that you're legally allowed. Most people overpay taxes every year simply because they don't know the law or what deductions are allowed. Large corporations have tax advisors helping them get the lowest tax bill possible, and so should you.

As a business owner for over 30 years, I can only offer you the knowledge that I've acquired over those years. Tax laws are always changing, and a CPA is required to continue their education on tax laws. They'll keep you up to date on current changes. Let them help you get the most benefit from tax regulations. A good accountant will make sure you only pay what is required and will ensure you receive all of the deductions allowed by law.

Create a list of your potential business deductions?

_____
_____
_____
_____
_____
_____
_____
_____
_____
_____
_____
_____
_____
_____
_____
_____
_____
_____
_____
_____
_____
_____
_____
_____
_____
_____
_____
_____
_____
_____

5

INSURANCE AND BONDING COVERAGE

LIABILITY INSURANCE

Liability Insurance, also known as general liability insurance, legally protects you if a customer experiences any damages, harm, or bodily injuries from the purchase of a product or service that you provide.

You might be thinking, do I really need it? My answer is, Yes! It's wise to carry liability insurance. Why take chances? You can build the cost of insurance into your job estimate or the product you're selling and pass it along to your customer, as most companies do! In most states, you will be required to have liability insurance in order to legally operate a business.

Being insured also gives the customer peace of mind that you are taking the proper precautions to protect your business. It makes a good selling feature when presenting your proposal. Having insurance will give you peace of mind, especially if you are a sole proprietor. As a sole proprietor, you won't have protection for your personal assets unless you do have insurance. Insurance covers the work or services and goods that you may provide.

Keep in mind, if your business requires you to go into someone's home to provide a service, you could get sued for damages if they were to occur. The same thing would apply to goods sold that could cause damages. It's just not worth the consequences. The most common lawsuits involve accidental events that occur on a client's property. Even though they're accidental, it doesn't change the fact that the customer could hold you liable if you break anything while working for them.

Let's face it: accidents happen! That's why they're called accidents. So, protect yourself and get insurance. You also might be thinking, "I'll just pay for it out of my own pocket if I break something while working." Sure, not having insurance might seem fine if you were to break a low-cost item, but what if the damage was extensive? That wouldn't be as easy to pay out of pocket. Plus, let's not forget, if the client wanted to get something for free out of it, they could sue you for not only the breakage of the item but could go for pain and suffering associated with the loss of an expensive, irreplaceable item. It's simply not worth it!

Get liability insurance. Shop around and get business insurance quotes from several agents in your area. Keep in mind that the policy with the lowest premium isn't always necessarily the best choice. Make sure you fully understand the coverage and exclusions you are receiving with your policy quote from each agent and then compare. Choose an agent you know will be there for you and who will design a policy that gives you the best protection if anything were ever to arise. Without insurance, one major loss could put you out of business.

BONDING

Is it necessary for you to get bonding for your business? This will depend on the type of business you are in. Usually it's not necessary unless you are an on-the-job-service type business like a cleaning service or contractor. Then it will be a good idea to protect yourself and your customers by having the bonding in place. Customers most often will not even ask you if you're bonded. They usually just ask about you or your employees and your business techniques.

There are two types of bond, fidelity and surety. A fidelity bond protects the clients you are working for from theft by you or by one of your current or past workers. This type of policy would only pay after there was a trial and someone was found guilty. Why customers like this type of bond is because it protects them in case your company is involved in any theft. The bond will cover you as the owner and all of your employees.

A bond can be purchased for one specific job or for several jobs. With a bond, if there is a theft or other damage, you can avoid the cost of going to trial in most cases, as the bond will cover the amount of the theft or other damage. If you operate your business reliably, you may not ever have to rely on the bond to cover losses, so, it may seem like an unnecessary expense but when you're bonded, prospective customers may be more comfortable choosing your business. Search for a bonding service with the lowest cost so you can have coverage even if you rarely have to use it.

The other type of bond you may need is a surety bond, also known as a performance bond. Most companies that provide services for individual homeowners will not need this type of bond. This type of bond is for higher-priced jobs. It basically guarantees the client you will perform the job you agreed to for the money you were requesting on the estimate given. It gives the customer the option to contact your insurance company and collect the funds necessary to complete the job if you were unable to. Your insurance company will then have to pay for these charges based on the terms of your policy.

As your company grows, you may find that you'll need other coverage. Here are some other types of insurance policies you may need as your business grows. See your insurance agent for full details.

- Property insurance: This covers your building and its contents, such as equipment or inventory, if it's damaged or if you experience a loss due to theft, or fire. Some policies have strict guidelines that must be followed, such as requiring security cameras, alarms, and fire suppression systems like sprinklers. If you haven't followed their guidelines and an incident occurs, then when you file a claim, they most likely will deny it! This is why it is so important to know and understand your policy.
- Workers' compensation insurance: This coverage is required by law when you have employees. However, if your employee happens to be your spouse, coverage for your spouse may not be required. Workers' compensation insurance provides coverage for your employees if they're injured on the job. Note: If you hire qualified workers as independent contractors and issue them a W-9 tax form at the end of the year, you may not be required to carry workers' compensation on them. However, you would want the independent contractor to carry their own insurance and provide you with a certificate of insurance to keep on file. This would be a yearly requirement and must not be overlooked for your protection.
- Commercial auto insurance: This is needed if you or your employees drive a company car or personal vehicle during the course of business. Large construction corporations, for example, will typically request that you carry at least a million-

dollar policy just to drive into their development or neighborhood while it is under construction if your business happened to be one of the trades working there. Each company is different and will require different policies based on their company's policies.

- Commercial crime insurance: Employee dishonesty coverage can help if employees steal from your company, whether on their own or with the help of outsiders.

"Provide, protect, and serve your customer with confidence."
- Tammy Mihalic

Keep your notes on Insurance quotes here

6

RECORD KEEPING

The most crucial part of running a successful business is maintaining good records. Good record keeping only makes good business sense. The key is to keep your records organized and simple right from the start of creating your business. With a few simple daily routines, rituals or habits to follow, you can be a successful bookkeeper in no time. With so, many amazing accounting programs to help you, it's almost impossible to fail. It only takes a little bit of effort on your part to create your system and follow it!

What should I be keeping records of, you may wonder? Everything! You'll want to keep a record of all income (accounts receivables) and expenses (account payable) coming in and going out of your business. You'll want to track exactly how much money you earn and spend. It is best to document your income as you receive it and your expenses as you incur them. Record who the money is from and what you spend your money on. Add dates and times of the transactions plus job-related details and all notes necessary to document that it was business-related. Save and document all receipts.

CASH OR ACCRUAL RECORD

There are two basic accounting systems a business can use to track and record income and expenses: cash or accrual. The best system for you will depend on the structure of your business, the volume of sales, and if you sell on credit or not.

The cash system is the simpler of the two methods. It records the actual cash that flows into and out of your business. The cash flows are the payments that come in and the expenses you pay out. The accounting date of record is the date you received your payment or paid out an expense, similar to the way you would maintain a personal check registry. This system is used by many sole proprietors, small service companies, and businesses with no inventory. This system can be beneficial from a tax standpoint at the end of the year because a business can record expenses right away while putting off recording their income until the following year. The cash system is a true record of what you are receiving and paying. It's simple and accurate!

The accrual system records payments and expenses on the date the transaction occurred instead of the date the money was actually paid or received. Meaning on the date you generate an invoice, you document that as income, and the day you order material, you document that as an expense. The term "accrual" refers to any single-entry recording income or expenses in the absence of a cash transaction. This system is used by businesses that maintain an inventory or those that sell on credit. Consult your CPA when deciding on which system to use.

INCOME RECORDS

Income records are the records or documentation you should keep on each client that pays you money. These records will tell who you billed, what you billed them for, how much you billed them, how they paid (check, cash, or credit), who made the payment, and the amount they paid. These are very important records that need to be kept. These records will tell you who hasn't paid and how long it took them to pay. Money owed is known as an outstanding balance. This information can be recorded on a simple chart or logged into an accounting program on your computer, which I recommend. Income record keeping is critical to running a successful business.

EXPENSE RECORDS

Expense records document how you are spending your money and how much is being spent. It is important to know where your money is going and how much you are spending. These records should be documented with the name and other relevant information of those you are paying money to. Record what job or customer it's for, the amount spent, plus the time and date the transaction took place. This, too, can be recorded on a simple chart or an accounting program on your computer.

CHECKBOOK RECORD

Your business checkbook is another form for documenting or recording your income and expenses, also called by some as your "ins and outs" or "debit and credit." This is your actual money. It's very important to keep a near-perfect record with your checkbook because you don't want to overdraft your account. To overdraw your account means you've attempted to spend money that you actually do not have in your checking account. If this were to happen, you would be charged a penalty for the mistake by your bank for as much as $45 per occurrence, or more, unless you have overdraft protection on your account, which I recommend. To ensure that this doesn't happen to you, make sure you record all money going in and coming out of your account on the very day it occurs and balance your checkbook every single month.

MILEAGE RECORD

Tracking your vehicles' mileage is required by the IRS in order to receive your automobile tax deduction. There is a standard mileage allowance that is used by everyone. This allowance could shortchange you if you're driving a gas hog. That is why you'll also want to keep and document all vehicle-related receipts. That total amount could then be deducted on your taxes as an actual expense at the end of that tax year as opposed to using the standard mileage rate to calculate your deduction. By not using the standard mileage allowance, you could possibly be able to take a higher deduction based on expenses.

Actual expense method: You keep track of and deduct all of your actual business-related expenses.

Standard mileage rate method: You deduct a certain amount (the standard mileage rate) for each mile driven for business, plus all business-related tolls and parking fees. The mileage rate is set by the IRS and is adjusted every year. You also might actually benefit from having a new car using the actual expense method, which allows you to deduct your vehicle's depreciation. Remember, only miles that were used for business are deductible. So, keep track of both personal and business use.

AUTOMOBILE EXPENSE RECORD

Expense records for your automobile will need to be kept. This record will prove to be valuable at tax time. Expenses to document will include car loan payments, license plate and registration fees, insurance, maintenance repairs, tires, tolls, parking, fuel, and car rentals would also apply. You must keep and maintain good records of all your receipts for proof of your spending. I recommend keeping a binder or labeled envelope for each month in your car or briefcase to keep such receipts and documentation. At the end of each month, bring them to the office for documentation and put into a permanent file that should be kept by the IRS guild lines of two years. This will really help you to stay organized and on top of your record keeping.

Recording or documenting as you go is much easier than going back at the end of the month or year, and trying to figure it out then. Take the time and record as you go. Don't forget to add any commuting miles traveled to meet a client, purchase business supplies, or to conduct research or work outside the office, or any other business-related activity.

"Keeping good records declutters the mind."
- Tammy Mihalic

CLIENT RECORDS

Client records are a way of keeping track of each client that you have given estimates to and have worked for. You'll need their legal name, job and billing address, home, cell, and work numbers, and email address. Having this information will be crucial if ever you had to sue for payment. You'll also record liens if filed, estimates and work performed, how much you billed and how they paid, and any outstanding balances, along with necessary notes. This profile will show if a client pays on time or is always late. This record shows a profile of the client's payment and work history, and will be beneficial for years to come.

MONTHLY NET INCOME STATEMENT

A monthly income statement is a record that documents your company's net income for each month. This record will show you your gross income first, followed by all of your company expenses. The difference between gross income and the total expenses of your company is your net income for the month. It is the perfect way to monitor and keep in check your company's increase or decrease in revenue and expenses. This statement will help you to know if a better budget should be implemented in any of the areas within your business. It's also great to use these figures to create a graph to look back on as the months go by to motivate you to do better with your business.

INVOICING RECORDS

Invoices are the dated bills given to each customer clarifying the work that you did for them and the amount charged, including your payment terms. An example of a payment term is that the invoiced amount is due in 30 days of the billing date, and a 10 percent late fee will be charged if not paid by the due date. Once paid, the invoice should be documented with the method of payment, the amount paid, and whether the invoice was paid in full or whether a balance is still due to you, and if the 10 percent late payment fee was applied.

You should make it your policy to collect upon completion of service once performed. Invoice and collect the same day you do the work, if possible. Let your clients know up front that this is your company's policy. This will save you from having to chase down your money or from having to go to court in the future. You can also collect a percentage upfront, then collect the balance upon completion of the service sold.

DAILY WORK SCHEDULE RECORD

A daily schedule should always be recorded and kept accurate. It is important to maintain a good detailed record of where you or your employees are working, what work was done, what materials were used, what time you arrived, how long it took to complete that job, and what time you left. Add any important information that you feel is necessary, such as whether anyone was hurt or if something was broken.

It's essential to maintain good records because it protects you. Make this a daily practice. The more details you put down, the better.

Doing this also helps you hone your estimating skills for future jobs and gives you a reference for your work timeline.

"Records are the memory of your business and protect your legal and financial interest."
- Tammy Mihalic

What helpful records can you start now for your business?

_____

_____

_____

_____

_____

_____

_____

_____

_____

_____

_____

_____

_____

_____

_____

_____

_____

_____

_____

_____

_____

_____

_____

_____

_____

_____

_____

_____

_____

7

SETTING UP YOUR OFFICE

When setting up your office, there are a few main things that should be considered: the location, control of noise, and lighting. Location is important because you'll want your office space to be someplace that you can actually sit down and focus on your work. Your space should be quiet and shouldn't be distracting. Believe it or not, a lot of distractions come from the location or layout of the office space and not because you lack focus.

Control of the noise around you is key to allowing your work energies to flow. Many times, I have seen a person's office crammed into a corner of a room with a TV blaring in another room, and they had no dedicated space. The location and noise control were awful.

When you work around loud, distracting sounds and are crammed into your workspace, you cram up your energy, thoughts, and creativity. You are cramming up your productivity and focus as well. Let's face it, we want our productivity to flow with ease when we are working. We get more done and are less frustrated when working in the right environment. So, when considering your office location, consider an open space with good flow and noise control.

Lighting is another important factor to consider when setting up your office. Without proper lighting, you can become tired, agitated, sluggish, or bored. You won't even realize that it was because of the lighting. Lighting can make or break your mood, which affects your ability to stay motivated and focused. Proper lighting can help you stay awake to get your work done in a timely manner too. I recommend bright lights for your workspace. Not only will you be able to see better to get your work done, but your mood and energy will stay amped.

Now that you're aware of the location, sound control, and lighting, let's look at the things you'll need to have for operating your office.

The most obvious is a desk. The desk doesn't have to be anything fancy—the simpler, the better, in my opinion. Practicality should be your key factor when considering a desk. A simple medium-sized office desk with a nice flat top, center drawer, two side filing cabinets, one on each side, with two additional top drawers is ideal for a good office desk. The key to a good desk is having what you need available, with easy, quick access, including ample tabletop space.

There are several options, such as an armoire desk unit. These are pretty, but not always functional and really don't offer much tabletop space. You could also use a dining or conference type table as your desk, provided you have a filing cabinet. The filing cabinet is one of the most important parts of maintaining an organized office. Even if you are keeping files digitally, you'll want a filing cabinet to keep hard copies. This will give you a clutter-free workspace! An organized clutter-free office means organized records, which means an organized business, which means an organized mind. An organized business keeps you efficient, and efficiency means saving time and earning more money easily and effortlessly.

In your office, you could be sitting for several hours at a time. Therefore, a comfortable chair is a requirement. You'll want to feel good while you're working, so, a good chair that supports your bum and back is highly recommended!

Besides having a cell phone, you'll also need a landline phone with an answering device, or you can hire an answering service. From experience, I know that people prefer a person answering the phone, not a machine. This should be a line for business calls only. You don't want to miss any customer's calls, do you? Every call has the potential to earn you money.

EQUIPMENT AND SUPPLIES REFERENCE LIST

- A separate phone line with an answering device
- Cell phone
- Simple desk or table
- Comfortable chair
- Filing cabinet
- Hanging file folders, label tabs and inserts
- Fireproof safe for storing important documents
- Computer, with an accounting program and Microsoft Office Suite
- Fax machine (Depending on your business, this can be useful.)
- Shredder to shred confidential documents
- Color Printer with scanner for printing letters, invoices, estimates, flyers, brochures, and for anything needing to be printed. (When printing in bulk, it's sometimes cheaper to hire a local printer to do the job.) The scanner is needed for getting documents, brochures, pictures, and other business-related items into your computer. You could also download a scanning

app on your smartphone, but the quality is usually not as professional looking. NOTE: *Many times, you can find a phone, scanner, printer, and fax machine all in one unit. This will consolidate your equipment and save desk space.*

- Ink or Toner
- 3-hole punch for documents and service manuals placed in three-ring binders.
- 3-ring binders
- Folders
- Envelopes (both letter and legal sizes)
- Stapler and staples
- Paperclips
- Pens, pencils, permanent markers, highlighters
- Backup USB drive
- Calculator
- Dry erase board with dry erasers
- Appointment book
- Wall and desk calendar
- Clipboard
- Copy paper
- Tablet paper
- Paper recycling bin
- Index cards
- Index page tabs
- Rolodex, or Contact Log, for all business contact names, phone numbers, and addresses. This can also be stored on your computer.
- Business card book to hold customer business cards.
- Post-it Notes
- Whiteout, to correct handwritten mistakes as needed.

WHAT WORK WILL YOU BE DOING IN YOUR OFFICE?

Your office is the most important part of your business, and the work you do here should be taken seriously. It's where you will start and end your day. It's here that you'll keep all legal documents, banking information, and business records (see Chapter 6: Record Keeping). It's essential for the health of your business to devote a few hours every day to your office duties. Here, you'll record and keep track of your business affairs while organizing and labeling documents to store in a filing cabinet and on your computer.

This is where you'll return phone calls. Write up estimates or proposals. Pay your bills or expenses. Record your income from those clients who have paid. Write up invoices to those who need to be billed. Send out reminder notices to those who haven't paid. Prepare deposits to be deposited at the bank, or do it online. Balance your checkbook. Go over all credit card charges and credits. Check business mail and emails. Post or respond to potential customers on social media. Work on new promotional money-making ideas. Look at your profit and losses. And always prepare the following day's schedule before leaving your office.

Revisit and meditate on your goals when you're in your office for at least five minutes a day. This would be a very good ritual to create and to follow. Reread your business plan and make any necessary changes that will help advance the growth of your business quickly. A successfully ran office keeps you organized, gives you peace of mind, and keeps more money in your pocket.

The key component to the success of any business is watching your money. Always be aware of where your money is and where it is going. Never pay someone else to govern your money in its entirety. If you find that you must hire an office accountant or bookkeeper to help you manage your money affairs, then it is very important to keep them within the boundaries you create. Setting boundaries for all employees is key, especially the person handling your money!

Make sure to create and enforce certain accounting steps. These steps must be taken when billing or receiving income, making bank deposits and withdrawals, and when purchasing supplies, materials, or product. One of these steps might include requiring a purchase order number (PO #) to be used for all purchases and returns of product or supplies. This can be set up with an accounting program on your computer and can also be documented in a logbook. This will allow you to track all purchases and returns more easily and will prevent a loss of money. When looking over receivables and payables, compare them to the work performed and materials used for that customer. Make sure they're priced correctly and can be referenced back to the PO # for that customer to ensure all material used for that job is priced right and is on that invoice. You may also have a separate payables bank account. If so, you would transfer money into that account from the main account as needed. This will protect the bulk of your money. Do not allow anyone but you to sign checks, and never spend your money without keeping track of it. Prevent embezzlement by never relinquishing full control over your money!

These simple acts of awareness will be vital when running your business. So, make it a part of your daily practice to always be aware of the money that you earn and spend in your business. Watch your own money, and pay everyone else to help you make it.

I've heard several horror stories from people who didn't keep proper tabs on their money. They placed too much trust in the person they hired to be in charge of their company's payable and receivable accounts. They didn't watch their money, nor did they set boundaries or have appropriate accounting procedures in place. They trusted the hired accountant, only to discover later the hired help was embezzling hundreds of dollars a week and, in some cases, thousands.

Stay aware of what is happening in your business. Do whatever it takes to get your business organized right from the start, and keep it that way! It's up to you as the business owner to develop a solid foundation on which to build your legacy! Keep it moving forward and stay in motion. The better you organize the monitoring and control of the company's money from the start, the better the rewards and profits in the end!

"Always stay aware of where your money is going in your business."
- Tammy Mihalic

KEEP YOUR WORKSPACE OFF-LIMITS TO OTHERS

Make it clear to everyone that your office space is off-limits to anyone except you, especially if your office is in your home. That means no spouse, children, friends, or neighbors should be in your office space at any time, unless for work. The office is a place to conduct your business and nothing else. Instruct your family and those in your household or place of business that when you're in your office, you're to be left alone. Zero disturbances while working means better productivity.

Your office stays private. You must maintain boundaries with family and friends. Treat your business office as you would any other professional place of business. This includes setting business hours. Give yourself a schedule to follow every day and stick to it! Keep your personal and business life in balance.

"Be productive! Set time limits for yourself."
- Tammy Mihalic

When your scheduled work time is over, get up and leave your office. Too much time in your office can lead to burnout, so, don't be tempted to work on personal matters while you're in your office. Set a different time and place for personal work. Avoid personal telephone calls or catching up on your personal emails during business hours.

Keep business work separate from your personal work. Don't use family or personal time to take care of business. Meaning, don't take your kids to the park and then stay on your phone conducting business instead of hanging out and playing with your children! You will find that keeping business, personal tasks, and family time separated is necessary to maintain a healthy balance of work and family in your life. Experiment with your work schedule to see what schedule will work best for you and your family; then, stick to it.

Use this space to create a list of business supplies you'll need

_____

_____

_____

_____

_____

_____

_____

_____

_____

_____

_____

_____

_____

_____

_____

_____

_____

_____

_____

_____

_____

_____

_____

_____

_____

_____

_____

_____

_____

_____

8

ADVERTISING AND MARKETING

Marketing is not the same as advertising. Advertising, however, is part of marketing. Marketing is done with the intent to get more customers for your business, by stimulating demand for goods or services; while targeting a select audience. Advertising is creating informative content illustrating and bringing attention to what it is you are selling. So, you must develop good communication skills with your potential customer! Marketing is figuring out what people want and then getting what they want to them. If you're only bringing people what they need and not what they want, they might not buy it no matter how you advertise to them. People are willing to pay for the things they want, even if that means spending more money for it.

Take, for example, cell phones. Yes, people feel that they need a cell phone, and there are several brands of cell phones and many models within a brand from which they can choose. However, because they *want* one particular model, they'll buy it and pay the extra money for it no matter what. Marketing is deciding how you will provide value and content that will fulfill a want and make people feel they can connect with your brand and your company to supply that desire.

First, when marketing, you'll need to answer these questions: What want or need are you addressing? What product or service can you provide that will fill that want or need? Who is your target audience? How can you get your target audience to notice and want to know about your product or service? What is your pricing strategy that will entice them to buy? What's in it for them? How will you deliver your product or service?

You'll need to carefully define the demographics of your targeted audience. Who are they, and why do they need your product or service? Where do they live or hang out? What is their age range? Their sex? Their income? How will your product or service make their lives better?

"If you're not putting out relevant content in relevant places, you don't exist."
- Gary Vaynerchuk

ADVERTISING

Advertising is developing and delivering public announcements to bring your product or service in front of the public with the intent of reaching potential customers, in order to draw attention to your business to promote sales. This also will be your time to show what sets your business apart from your competition. There are both free and paid means of advertising that can be delivered through multiple types of media or platforms. Word of mouth is the most powerful form of advertising. Other ways to advertise are flyers, blog posts, newspapers, radio, mail inserts or postcards, interviews, podcasts, the Internet (social media), Google Ads, Groupon, TV and radio commercials, magazines, billboards, etc.

You'll need to figure out how you will introduce your products or services to the world as well as how to promote the identity (the brand) of your business. How will you capture the attention of the public eye? You will have to decide what is best for you and the amount of money you wish to spend.

An advertising budget for a person starting out in business with zero to one or two employees will be much different from someone who already has a large established business with lots of employees. Whether it is a small or large business, the goal of advertising is to gain and retain enough customers to keep the business running and profitable.

Advertising can be free or cost very little if you use websites like Craigslist, Offerup, Nextdoor, Linkedin, Facebook Market Place, Pinterest and YouTube or write posts on social media sites. It can also be inexpensive to list an ad on these sites or in some of your local papers.

You could also spend hundreds or thousands of dollars through other sources like magazines, television commercials, and billboards in your area of business. Normally what you spend will be determined by how quickly and how big you want your business to grow.

A good question to ask yourself as a new business owner is how quickly and how big do you want to grow? The answer will help determine your advertising budget. If you are operating your business alone, you may wish to advertise only enough to keep your work schedule full. If you have employees or intend to hire some because you are ready to expand your business, then you'll want to spend more on advertising until you've reached your desired size.

Although having demand greater than supply may be a good problem to have, be careful not to advertise in a way that generates demand faster than your ability to supply it. It wouldn't make any sense to advertise if you couldn't supply enough product or have the bandwidth to deliver services to meet the demand. That would hurt your reputation!

"Stopping advertising to save money is like stopping your watch to save time."
- Henry Ford

Anytime you interact with people, let them know about your business. Ask if they could use your services and give them a business card. Ask people for referrals! People really do like helping other people, but you have to ask! Ask places of business if they can use your services and ask if you can leave flyers or business cards with them. Remember to always stay excited about your business! You are, after all, living the American Dream of having your own business.

Besides advertising by word of mouth, you can advertise by placing an ad in your local newspapers or print up flyers and deliver them door-to-door or hand them out as you meet and greet people. Place an advertising pamphlet with companies that provide monthly mail inserts. Talk to your local radio stations and run a radio spot on both AM and FM stations in your community. Check with your cable provider about running commercials on your local cable stations. Plus, let's not forget the Internet and all social media sites and YouTube. With YouTube, you can create a free account and create videos about you and your business and post them regularly for free. Your friends on social media can advertise for you by simply posting your business on their page and recommending it to their friends and followers. A large percentage of businesses generate sales from a customized website, so, you should consider creating a professional-looking online presence. This will not only help to generate sales, but it gives you the opportunity to offer detailed information about you and your business.

Keep in mind that some advertising, such as TV, can be costly and not necessarily cost-effective for a business that's just starting out, unless you're planning to grow and expand your business by leaps and bounds.

One of the best ways to advertise when starting out is to first advertise to those you know. Let friends, family, neighbors, and other associates like your dentist, doctor, hairstylist, insurance agent, and even your local butcher know that you've started a business and are looking for clients.

Ask them for their help. Most people are willing to help if you ask. So, ask! Ask them if they would hire you or help you spread the word about your new business. This is a great way to get started. Need more exposure? Try putting up a flyer on your local store's community boards.

Most importantly, get a business card! You can order them online or have a local printing company make them. Your card should list your name, the business's name, your business phone number, email address, website, your logo if you have one, and the product or service you are providing. You can also provide your license number and your insurance or bonding information if that is customary for your service. A photo of yourself is optional but works great in helping people to remember you, and I highly recommend it.

Want free advertising? Then make an impact on everyone you meet by talking about your business with enthusiasm and excitement. Let them know how much you love your business and like helping people. Let them know your desire to grow, and ask if they'd help you by spreading the word.

"Doing business without advertising is like winking at a girl in the dark. You know what you are doing, but nobody else does."
- Stewart Henderson Britt

MARKETING

Marketing is the most important part of a business, and you should invest a good amount of time in determining your best marketing strategies. It's all about the power of positioning yourself amongst those you are competing against in your niche'. Now is the time for you to figure out your Unique Selling Proposition (USP). Having a clear vision for your USP is a key element to branding your business, product, or services. To help you to discover your USP, you will need to have the answers to a few questions. What is it about your company or products that makes you different or sets you apart from others like you? What one thing about your business is unique and makes you stand out from your competition? What highlights the benefits of your business that will be meaningful to the consumer?

When advertising, you must make an emotional proposition to the consumer. Why will they benefit from your business or from using your product? Your proposition should be different from what your competition is offering. Create a strong proposition that inspires consumers to become your customer. Consumers are looking for a business that offers services that no one else offers. How does your ideal customer benefit from working with you versus your competition?

To help you to determine your USP, make a list of what your business does or services it provides. Then cross out the things your competition does that your business also does. There will be certain aspects of your business that will be the same; those are universal selling proposition that everyone in your line of business does. Your USP must be desirable to others. People buy what they want; you must tell them what they need, and then it can become a must-have! What do people want from your business, and are they willing to pay for it? What makes your business so valuable that people would pay double for it? What specific benefit does it offer? Describe that benefit! What could your business do that would be unique, desirable, and specific to your customers? Shift your thinking from a business view to a consumer's view. Look at your business through the eyes of the consumer to determine what they need or want from you. Then brainstorm on how to give that!

Let's take pizza companies, for example. Every pizza place sells pizza, and all pizza is basically the same—dough, sauce, and toppings. So when Domino's Pizza was created, they had to figure out their USP. How were they going to get the public to want their pizza over the competition's pizza? That is when Domino's Pizza came up with their speedy delivery service. They made a promise to deliver your pizza in 30 minutes or less, or it would be free! That caused a lot of consumers to become customers for two reasons—they got their pizza delivered faster to their door, and they knew if it was late, they'd get it for free! Do you see how Domino's found their unique selling proposition and set their company apart from the others?

Once you have determined your USP, you can direct your energies toward creating your marketing plan. To help you develop your plan, let's look at the four Ps of Marketing. The four basic Ps of Marketing are: Product, Price, Promotion, and Place.

- **First P: Product.** What product or service are you selling, and what makes it unique among your competitors? (This is your USP.)
- **Second P: Price.** What price will you be selling your product or service for? Establishing an effective pricing strategy will ensure good profits.
- **Third P: Promotion.** Once product and price are determined, you can promote. Promotion is the way you brand your business and make your product or service known to the world. Advertising is just one component of promotion. You'll want to position your brand to receive maximum return.
- **Forth P: Place**. Where will your customers look for your product or service? If you have a new product, consider what type of stores will best showcase it. Find the ideal place to find potential customers and engage them with your business to convert them into customers.

"Master the topic, the message, and the delivery"
- Steve Jobs

Establishing your marketing plan is just the beginning. It doesn't stop there! As a business owner, you'll always be marketing and engaging your potential targeted customers. Your message should inspire them with a feeling of trust and confidence in your performance and ethics when selling your products or services. When talking about your business, express how happy you are to serve them. Be different and stand out from your competition. Always greet people with a happy smile and a good attitude. Keep a sparkling, clean car. Maybe wear a clean and tidy uniform, or have an outstanding sales presentation.

First impressions start with the introduction of your business right from that first phone call made or first advertisement placed. Communicate the feeling of why your products or services are different from the other companies. Give them the feeling that by engaging with your company, they'll get more! Leave the impression that you're trustworthy and have the knowledge and capabilities to meet all of their needs. Make them feel confident in hiring your company.

After meeting with a potential customer, make sure that you do a follow-up phone call, email, or drop a postcard in the mail. Let them know that you were happy to meet them and thank them for considering your company. Your follow-up could be the very thing that converts them into a paying customer. So, always check back with them a few days after your initial meeting. This type of follow-up has landed me many customers that I would've lost to my competitors had I not done it. As a rule of thumb: if you didn't gain a customer the first time around, don't lose hope! You can still get that potential customer by doing another follow-up, either on the phone or maybe in person a few weeks later. Oftentimes, that customer will find they're not happy with their current company and will give you a chance to win their business. The right marketing is making your business or

0product stand out from your competition by doing things that the other guy won't do. It's about getting people to view your product or service as something better and more valuable than your competitors. Never be afraid to be different from the rest. Be your unique self. It will pay off in the long run! Keep the faith!

"Strong propositions inspire consumers to become your customer."
- Tammy Mihalic

SOCIAL MEDIA

In today's digital world, a company should create and maintain an engaging online presence, not to mention, create, the perfect digital marketing strategy. The Internet is everyone's go-to place when they want to know about things, people, or a business. If you or your company's name cannot be found through a Google search, you could potentially lose business.

If you don't want to create a costly website now, no worries! You have a few ways to create an online presence for your company by using popular social media sites like LinkedIn and Alignable, which are made specifically for business owners. Then you have the others like Nextdoor, Pinterest, Rumble, SafeChat, YouTube Instagram, and Facebook. Sites like these will allow you to create your company's online presence for free! These sites are also a great place to buy advertising to get the word out about your business locally or globally.

It's a great way to inform your community about you, your company, and the work you perform.

With social media being the wave of our future, you'll want to be on at least one of these free popular online sites. These sites will give customers a place to visit to learn more about you and your company. You can post pictures of yourself and the work you do or the things you sell. There, you can blog, create inspirational content, and offer useful information like advice or solutions from your company that can benefit the reader.

The purpose of these sites is to give potential clients the opportunity to get to know you. When someone feels like they know you, it builds trust. When people feel they can trust you, they'll be more likely to buy what you're offering.

"Social Media: Engage, Promote, Inspire, Create, Influence, Connect."
- Tammy Mihalic

What will be your unique selling proposition and marketing plan?

9

CREATING A COMPANY SERVICE MANUAL

Once you have decided how you're going to operate your business and which services or goods you plan to offer your community, you'll want to write things out in detail in what is known as a service manual. Although you may not deem it necessary to write out this information in a manual, know that you are actually creating an organizing tool for yourself and the company you'll be forming. This manual will not only aid you in how you're operating your business, but it will also educate your potential customers about your policies and services offered.

A well-written service manual can become your greatest selling tool when bidding jobs. This will also be your tool to refer back to if your customer was to forget any of your policies. A service manual is worth its weight in gold!

Now, the type of business you decide to go into will determine if you really do need or want a service manual. Oftentimes, service-orientated companies that present a yearly contract, such as landscapers, contractors, pool cleaners, etc., will find a manual very useful. A store owner or hair salon may deem it unnecessary to create one. However, because it contains valuable information about your business's policies and operations, you may find it useful for your own personal use.

WHAT IS A SERVICE MANUAL?

A service manual tells everyone, in writing, what your business is all about. It informs, in detail, the services and operational policies that you're providing to your customer and what you are expecting from them. It impresses upon them the importance of your business and that you're professional and serious about your business. It shows you value your reputation, are in it for the long haul, and are up front about your business policies. First impressions matter! Your service manual also sets your business apart from other companies in your industry.

CREATING YOUR COMPANY'S MANUAL

- A service manual will fully explain the services that you do and do not provide.
- In the service manual, you'll discuss your billing and payment policies, including when payment is due, whether there are late payment penalties, and if interest is charged on outstanding balances. Plus, you should remember to state the penalties that will be charged on bounced checks.
- You should also provide a section of frequently asked questions. This shows your customers that you're aware of their concerns and needs.

- Some of these frequently asked questions should cover details about the products or services you offer. This is your opportunity to let your customers know that you collect payment at the time the services are rendered. Cash flow is the most important part of any business. So, it's very important to let all customers know that you get paid the day a service is performed. The service manual will also contain your contact information.

- A service manual goes by other names such as a business handbook, business guide, or policies and procedures handbook. It will become a selling tool for your business. It will state what you're willing to provide and at what cost. It'll eliminate any future confusion if customers claim they weren't aware of your policies.

- You can also create a service manual or business handbook for newly hired employees. These written policies create boundaries and clarify what is expected of your employees and help you hold them accountable. This could also be used as a tool to defend your company if an employee sues or tries to file for unemployment benefits after being fired for misconduct.

HOW SHOULD I DRAFT MY MANUAL?

In this section, I'll go over some of the typical information that will go into your service manual. Of course, you can add more or take away items as you choose according to the type of business you'll be operating. It's *your* company's policies, so the decision is up to you. I'll include a sample of what a service manual may look like to help you when you are creating your own. Feel free to follow my guidelines if you choose.

Your service manual could be emailed or printed out, put in a folder, and then hand-delivered. The folder's two pockets can be used for any additional information, like promos or coupons that you may be offering for that month or later in the year. It can also be a place to leave your estimate for a job proposal or a place to staple your business card.

People are visual creatures. Placing your manual in a folder will make for a better presentation of your company. This will set you apart from businesses competing in your industry.

THE COVER PAGE

The first page of your manual will be your cover page. It will be the first page people will lay their eyes on. This page should be kept simple. Keep it neat and clean. Don't clutter this page with unnecessary information. It should only contain the name of your business, address, and all contact information. Followed by a tagline and the main information about the purpose and vision of your business, also known as a mission statement.

Choose and place in the header of your cover page one of the following titles. This will clue your customers to be aware of what it is they are reading.

Here are some title options for you to choose from for your manual:

- Service Manual
- Business Manual
- Business Policy

- Service Policy
- Business Handbook
- Service Handbook
- Business Guide
- Service Guide

WHAT GOES IN YOUR COMPANY'S SERVICE MANUAL?

- Business name in large print
- Address
- Phone number, including area code
- Email address
- Web presence information such as website URL, LinkedIn, Facebook, Instagram, Pinterest, etc.
- Logo, if you have one
- A tagline and mission statement that captures the nature of your company. *Examples of taglines may look something like*: "Serving your community since 1988," or "House sitting for homes since 1988." Think of a simple tagline that best represents you, and how you can make their life better by hiring you. These are not a sales pitch but are only a catchy statement that represents your business. *You will also write a paragraph that states why you are in business*. This is why you're doing what you're doing. It can be the reason behind your cause. This is what's known as a mission statement. Almost all successful companies will have one. This will be placed on the bottom of the cover page.
- Company Policies and information
- Work or services you will provide, followed by a customer contract

CREATING YOUR MISSION STATEMENT

This mission statement tells your customer why you're doing what you're doing in a fun and meaningful way that allows you to be seen in the most favorable light. The reasons why you created your company will help determine your success. People will see that you're genuine and have a purpose for what you're doing besides earning money. It's a good idea for all businesses to have a mission statement. It helps the potential customer relate to you and your reason for why you're in business.

This statement is not about money or the money you'll get from being in business. It's more about your cause or purpose as to why you are doing what you're doing—it's your reason for being in business. It's about the satisfaction of that good feeling you get from helping people.

Your mission statement will help people to connect with you. It will show people that your main objective for being in this business is to serve them and why that's important to you. This is a time for you to express your personality with the business you operate. Be what you say you are and nothing else! Plus, be sure to read several other company's mission statements for inspiration to help you to create your own.

HERE IS AN EXAMPLE OF A MISSION STATEMENT:

Our Mission

Celebrating life by helping others.

Here at Golden Touch House Sitting, our mission is what guides our culture and our uncompromising commitment to quality service for our customers. When knowing your home isn't alone really matters to you, trust Golden Touch House Sitting.

ENHANCE YOUR WORDS

Enhance your words! What do I mean by that? Upgrade them a notch or two. There is power in our words and the way we use them. So, use your words to help express who it is you are. Use your words to educate and uplift! Our words can build us up or tear us down. So, choose words that will build you and your company up when expressing your work values.

Here are some examples of what I mean by enhancing your words:

- Instead of using the word "cheap," replace it with the word "affordable." So, instead of saying, "We offer cheap rates!" which makes your business sound cheap, replace it with, "We offer affordable pricing!" Everyone relates to the word "affordable" as a sign of fair pricing.
- Instead of, "We are experienced house sitters!" replace the word "experienced" with "professional." "We are professional house sitters!" See how changing one word makes you look more legitimate? Changing "experienced" to "professional" shows

the customer you are knowledgeable and serious about your business.

- Instead of saying, "We are pleased to serve you," replace "pleased" with the word "committed." "We are committed to serving you." The word "committed" tells the customer that you value their business and that you're in it for the long haul!
- Instead of saying, "We want to offer you great service with every house." say, "Our goal is giving you quality service with every house."

So, give it a shot and have fun while creating your manual! Play around with it. Read it out loud. Ask for the opinion of family and friends. Most will be glad to help you. Ask around your community and research other company's mission statements to help you with your own.

EXISTING CUSTOMER BASE

This section of your service manual will show your new customers who you're already servicing and what type of work you're doing for them. New clients like to see who else you're already working for. It gives them assurance that you'll provide a good service for them as well.

So, you might say something like, "I house-sit for homes for families with children and pets. Some of my clients are the busy bachelor types who find themselves needing to leave town on the spur of the moment and know they can count on me with short notice. Others plan out their yearly vacations and schedule me a year in advance."

This section is important because it'll show your new customer other houses that you're sitting for. This will also be beneficial when it comes to customer referrals.

INITIAL CUSTOMER MEETING

This section of your manual describes what the customer can expect at the first meeting, such as what you'll talk about and how much time you'll need with them. This will be their time to discuss and go over their needs and to get answers to all the questions and concerns that they may have for you.

This meeting is essential! You'll define exactly what you will and will not be doing for that customer.

SERVICES PROVIDED

In this section of your manual, you will give a brief description of what you'll provide for your customer and what you will not. This is your time to speak up and set your boundaries and expectations that come with your services. It is much easier to explain now what comes with your service as opposed to after you start working for them! This section will give clarity in writing about the work you will provide. This will be helpful for both you and for the customer to refer back to if a question about your services were to ever arise.

EXAMPLE FOR A HOUSE-SITTING BUSINESS:

- No one is to be in the home other than you.
- A/C is to be kept at 77 degrees.
- Mail deliver will be stopped.
- What happens if you're late or need to reschedule?
- What happens if they need to reschedule?
- Are there charges applied if the customer cancels?
- Are there discounts if you have to cancel?

PRIVACY, SECURITY, AND SAFETY

When operating a service type business, like house sitting, you'll be going into a lot of people's homes. So, it's very important that your customers know that their personal lives will remain private. This is your time to reassure them that their privacy is of the utmost importance to you.

Security is another important factor for the homeowner. You'll be given a key, and they need to know that their home is safe. You'll need to let them know that their key and house information is safe with you and that their key is locked in a safe place on the days you are not sitting for their home. The safety of your customer's home should be your number one priority. You, or they, could also provide a lockbox that will hold their house key, and will be kept on the premises.

Use this section of the manual to state that you will not work with other service providers while you're taking care of their property due to security concerns or the risk that one or both may get hurt when working together, unless this is a part of your hired work duties. State any safety concerns here in this section of your manual.

114

EMAIL LIST AND SOCIAL MEDIA

Creating an email list is important to any business, along with connecting on social media. When you ask for an email address or for social media contact information, let the customer know that you are creating these connections so, you can send out newsletters, promotions, alerts, holiday or vacation reminders, or even birthday wishes. You might even use the database to get their support for events that you may be taking part in, like your annual 5K Run for Feed the Children or a fundraiser to save an animal from a kill shelter. This shows your customer that you're involved in your community and you care, also, let the customer know that their email is for your use alone and will not be sold or abused in any way.

COMMUNITY EVENTS AND CHARITABLE CAUSES

This is your chance to convey how much you value specific community events and to talk about your involvement with them. This is your prime time to express the value that you hold for your favorite charity and that a percentage of your business proceeds go to this charity. Express to your potential client which organizations you give to. They may very well support the same charity and feel a bond with you and hire you for your services just for that reason. Remember, your giving to others will go a long way. Consider giving as seeds sewn for your future wealth!

Operating days and hours are the days and hours your business will be opened for service for hire. In order to have a productive workday or workweek, you will want to keep a good work schedule and stick to it! Scheduling is the most important part of your business. Without a well-maintained schedule to follow, your company will be disorganized. This means losses. As a business owner, you do not want that. If your business requires driving, schedule your jobs in a geographical order if possible and within time restraints. This will save you wear and tear on your vehicle, fuel, and time, which means more money in your pocket at the end of the day! In this section, you will provide clients with the days and times you will be available.

"Always utilize your time efficiently!"
- Tammy Mihalic

Distance also is a factor to consider. If your business requires you to travel, I'd recommend scheduling the farthest job away from your starting point as your first appointment in the morning, if possible. This way, you'll find yourself back closer to home when your workday is done. If you have children to come home to or that are involved in sports or after-school activities, this will allow you to participate because you'll be finishing up with work close to home. However, if you find that it is simpler to do the farthest job away last, then do so. It's your business, so schedule it the way that works best for you.

CANCELLATION AND RESCHEDULING POLICY

Here you'll describe what you expect if your clients need to cancel or reschedule. Will fees apply? Will you be able to reschedule them that same week? Or will the schedule continue as normal? This section should cover both you and the customer if the need was to arise that either one needed to cancel or reschedule. This section will also cover what happens if contracts are canceled, what type of penalty would apply, or how many days' notice either party should give before canceling and why.

BILLING AND PAYMENTS

This will be the most important part of your service manual because it has to do with collecting money. <u>Your money!</u> Without it, you're not in full control. Cash flow is the most fundamental part of any business. It's important to bill your customer and receive payment as soon as possible upon completion of each job. This cannot be emphasized enough! Customers normally will not have any problem paying you upon completion of your services.

In this section, you'll let the customer know how you bill and collect for your services rendered and what forms of payment you accept. (Cash, Credit Cards, Checks) Most companies bill and collect upon completion of the job, but you may find billing bi-weekly or monthly is easier to keep track of, while collecting your money every 30 days.

If you accept checks, you will need to state the fees charged if you were to receive a check that bounced due to them having insufficient funds. This will also, be the time to mention they will incur a fee if payment is paid past the 30-day due date. As a business owner you will have the option to charge a monthly fee or an interest rate on the overdue amount. Interest rates normally range from 1% to 1.5%. These fees are normally only charged to a customer who refuses to pay after several attempts to collect the funds. Always call a customer first with a gentle reminder that payment is past due. After several documented attempts to collect your money is when you would resend a bill with the late fee attached.

Credit cards are a great form of payment to offer your clients and are recommended. Just remember, when offering your client, the convenience of paying with a credit card, there are processing fees you must pay on the percentage of the amount collected. These charges normally range between three and seven percent. That means you will receive less that amount of what you charged your customer when they pay by credit card.

If you choose to offer credit cards as a form of payment, you could pass the expense on to the client but would need to inform them that you're doing that up front. Only you can decide if accepting credit cards as a form of payment and passing that expense on to the customer makes sense for your business.

You'll find that if you create boundaries with your customers, they'll respect you more and will abide by them. However, this must be done upfront. (This same policy of boundary setting should also apply to employees when you hire them!)

Boundaries are a great way to keep your business in check. When working for a business or under a commercial contract, you can apply the same boundaries. Tell them that you expect payment upon completion of the job. Most will comply; however, on occasion, you'll have a larger company that may not be willing to comply with your billing and payment requirements. For example, when you are doing several jobs a week, they may require you to bill all of your jobs together. Large establishments normally have a cutoff day for billing, and they may pay only once a month or biweekly. This type of accounts payable policy is convenient, provided you stay on top of billing and collecting your money.

Collecting is just as important as billing and must be done in a timely fashion. Never get lazy in your accounting department, never! Collect your money as soon as you can. Remember these three accounting rules to keep your business affairs flowing smoothly and stress free: Bill on time. Collect on time. Pay on time.

COMPANY RATES AND FEES

Company Rates and Fees should be placed toward the back of your manual. You want your customer reading all about your business and getting to know you first before talking about the rates that you charge for your services.

Doing this allows them to know who they're hiring and will provide them with the much-needed information they're looking for. Here, you'll state the duration of your rate and when the contract expires. State your weekend and holiday rates along with emergency rates for when they need you at the last minute. Now would be a good time to mention if there will be any renewal increases due to inflation and what percentage that may be.

You'll also state whether discounts are available for promotions or referrals.

RENEWING CONTRACTS

This important section of your manual is to make sure that your customers are aware of when the contract date starts and expires. You'll want to clearly state your price and how long that price is good: six months, one year, etc.

Contracts can ensure your company's stability because you know that you have guaranteed work for that amount of time. When it's time to renew a contract, you'll have the opportunity to increase your rates and to make any changes that may be needed, such as adding or taking away a service. This also gives you an out to stop doing business with a customer who is tougher to deal with than expected without it tarnishing your reputation!

GENERAL INFORMATION

This section of your manual covers the qualifications of your company. Here you'll show your insurance and bonding information along with your policy numbers, coverage amounts, and the names and numbers of your providers. Your business license number and contact information can be in this area as well, along with any other general information you'd like to supply.

DETAILS

This very important section of your manual will give you and your customer the details of your services and what you plan to provide. If questions or concerns were ever to arise about what services you provide, you'll have this detailed sheet to refer back to.

It's important not to rush yourself during this step. The information you provide in this section allows your potential customer the opportunity to get acquainted with your company, which will give you a better chance of getting their business.

"Defining details now will spare you from arguments or grief later."
- Tammy Mihalic

Golden Touch House Sitting

www.Goldentouchhousesitting.com

email: Sally@Goldentouchhousesitting.com

1111 Heavens St

Paradise Beach, FL 77777

777-777-7777

Creating peace of mind for each vacationing homeowner since 1977.

Thank you for allowing Golden Touch House Sitting the opportunity to serve you with all of your home sitting needs!

My Mission Statement

Golden Touch House Sitting has been happily providing quality house sitting for homes since 1977. My mission is to ease the homeowner's mind in knowing their home is safe and cared for while they're away from home.

Contact Information

All inquiries may be directed to my phone at 777-777-7777 or email at: Sally@GoldenTouchHouseSitting.com

Thank you! You are receiving this service manual because you are considering or have already hired Golden Touch House Sitting Services to be your personal helper in keeping your home safe and cared for while you're away. I personally want to thank you for the trust you've place in us.

Existing Customer Base

Golden Touch House Sitting specializes in residential house-sitting needs. We currently sit for a variety of individuals ranging from elderly individuals to families with children who reside in houses, apartments, condos, and modular homes ranging from 440 square feet to as large as 7700 square feet. No house-sitting job is too big or too small.

We serve a clientele of repeat customers. Some may need us for as much as eight months out of the year or as little as a weekend getaway. Some give us advance notice, which is much appreciated. However, we also have flight attendants who, many times, need to call on our services at the last minute. Either way, we are there for all of our customers.

Initial Customer Meeting

We will meet all of our prospective clients at the location of the house to be sat for. One of our professionals or the owner of Golden Touch House Sitting, Sally Goldstein, will conduct the meeting. The meeting will generally last 20 to 40 minutes, so, please allow for adequate time when scheduling.

(Please have all questions or concerns ready prior to our meeting.)

At the meeting, we'll discuss and do the following:

1. Initial meet and greet.
2. Discuss overall needs and concerns and answer any questions.
3. Walk through each room to familiarize the company with your home.
4. Show location of electrical panel, water and gas main shut-off valves.
5. Discuss business operation policies, scheduling, and payments.
6. Discuss key or entry arrangements.
7. Review services to be rendered.
8. Fill out contract information.
9. Sign and date contract.
10. Leave folder and a copy of the contract with the customer. Originals stay with company files.

We here at Golden Touch value meeting with all new potential clients to discuss and evaluate their home sitting needs. We recognize that not all clients are a match. We reserve the right to decline services as we deem appropriate.

Services Provided and What to Expect:

- Please count on a team member to visit your home daily as scheduled.
- All mail and packages brought inside and placed in the agreed-upon location.
- Home to be walked through and monitored as per contract agreement.
- Keys and security codes will always be kept secure, safe, and private.
- Your private information will always be kept completely confidential.

- After service is rendered, we will meet again to exchange the bill for payment and return the key.

What Golden Touch Expects From a Customer:

- All toys, clothes, or other living items picked up off the floors and in walk areas.
- No pets to be left at home. (Pet sitting services are provided at an additional expense. See service provider for details.)
- No children or teens are to be left unsupervised. (Childcare services are provided at an additional expense. See service provider for details.)
- No other vendors are to be allowed in the home while you're away unless preapproved.
- Windows and doors to remain closed and locked.
- Adequate air conditioning or heating in the home, depending on the season.
- Running water and electricity are available.
- Provide automated timers for lighting in the home. This will give the appearance that someone is home. (Automated timers are available for purchase at $39)

NOTE: Service could be refused if expectations are not met.

Golden Touch Will Not:

- Answer your door or phone or check your answering machine.
- Go through your mail or packages.
- Go through your personal items.
- Clean your home. (Cleaning services are provided at an additional expense. See service provider for details.)

Privacy / Security / Safety

- Here at Golden Touch, we value our customers and want you to know your privacy is of utmost importance to us. None of your home or family information is shared. Whatever happens in your home stays in your home.
- Security is important to us all. That is why when we're in your home, doors will be locked behind us upon entering to do our walk-through and will be locked when we leave.
- Safety measures are taken in all homes.

Email List and Social Media

Here at Golden Touch, we have created an email and social media contact list so, we can send out special promos, holiday and vacation reminders, or birthday wishes. Please know that your information will never be sold or shared.

Community Events and Charitable Causes

At Golden Touch, a portion of our net proceeds goes to the "Save a Life, Make a Friend Foundation," which is an organization focused on saving animals from local kill shelters and finding them good homes. Our team also participates in their Special 5K race, which happens every March to help raise money to save the lives of animals from our local kill shelters. All customers who are interested in participating or would like to know more about "Save a Life, Make a Friend" please contact the owner, Sally Goldstein, for details.

Operating Days / Hours and Scheduling

- Golden Touch operates daily from 7:00 a.m. to 7:00 p.m.
- Scheduling is worked geographically based on workload.

Cancellation and Rescheduling Policy

- Cancellation by the customer requires a 72-hour notice, or there is a penalty charge of $45, unless the reason for cancellation is an act of God.
- Golden Touch will honor the same policy if we were to cancel without giving a 72-hour notice and will pay you $45, unless it's an act of God.
- Rescheduling of any cancellation will be done based on availability.

Billing and Payments

- All jobs are billed and payment is expected upon completion of job.
- All 30 day past due balances are subject to a 1.5 percent monthly late fee.
- A fee of $55 will apply to all insufficient checks as per company regulations.
- Payment by credit card is subject to a 6 percent credit card processing fee.

Company Rates and Fees

- Each job will be priced individually and worked according to contract.
- Holiday and emergency rates are higher.
- All rates are good for six months, not including holidays.
- Discounts or coupons must be presented at the time of estimate and cannot be applied to past work performed.

Renewing Contracts

- All contracts should be renewed 30 days prior to expiring to avoid delays in scheduling or service. Renewal increase of 1 to 5 percent based on inflation.

General Information

License #777777-77

General Liability and Bonded by:

Heavensake Insurance Company

PO BOX 77777

Miami, FL 77777

#111-111-1111

Customer's Home Details

- Each room will be walked into to ensure all things are safe and sound.
- Team member will look for any unusual activity inside and outside the home and will make sure everything in the house stays in good working order.
- A/C will remain at 78 degrees unless otherwise stated by homeowner.
- Water to bathrooms and all sinks except the kitchen will be shut off.
- Water heater to be placed in vacation mode.
- **Please see attachments for any additional notes or add them here.**

*Sample Customer Contact Page and House-Sitting Details

Date _____

Customer Name _James and Jean Doe_ Email jimjean@gmail.com

Cell # _111-111-1111_ Home # Work number _____

Address _77 Golden Street_ _____

City Royal Heights _____ State _FL_____ Zip Code ___77777_

Family Members Names _Sally Doe, daughter_ _____

Pets and their names _Angel the dog_ _____

Alarm system?   YES _X_ NO   Security Name and Number

Security Code and Instruction_____

_____

_____

Key Holders and Entry Detail: _Key will be given to team member prior to start date for service or at the time of signing the contract agreement. Door will be locked upon exiting. Key will be returned to homeowner after returning from trip and collecting service fee._

Emergency Contacts

Name _Jean Doe_____Name _____

Number _333-333-3333_____Number _____

Relation _Wife_____Relation _____

Contract Agreement Signature Page

House Sitting Start Date: _July 07, 2027_ through to Finish Date: _July 15, 2027_ I, _James Doe_____have read and agreed to the terms and conditions of this contract for the Price of: _____$200__

_____

Payment is due in full upon completion of finish date.

You also agree if payment is not rendered and legal actions were required to collect funds, you acknowledge that you will pay for all of Golden Touch legal fees, court cost, and accumulated interest.

_____initial

_____   _____

Customer Signature   Contract Date

_____   _____

Estimator's Signature   Contract Date

What information will you need in your Service Manual?

_____

_____

_____

_____

_____

_____

_____

_____

_____

_____

_____

_____

_____

_____

_____

_____

_____

_____

_____

_____

_____

_____

_____

_____

_____

_____

_____

_____

_____

_____

_____

10

CUSTOMERS AND YOUR WORTH

Now that you have everything in place and are ready to get started taking customers or orders, the next question is, how do you find your customers? For some people, this is the most difficult part of starting their new venture. But it goes without saying: In order to get business, you must let people know that you're in business. If no one knows that you have started a business, then they will not be able to hire you for your services, buy your goods, or recommend you to others.

Be proud that you're in business for yourself, and make sure to sign up with the Better Business Bureau and your City's Chamber of Commerce. This is one thing many businesses fail to do, but it is the perfect way to get to know other important people in your community. Besides, it will help you advertise your business to not only the residence in your area but other local business owners as well. Don't be shy about your business! Stand in confidence. You have taken charge of your destiny. Own it! Get excited! Be enthusiastic and share your business with everyone you meet.

When you convey this type of happy enthusiasm, not only will people take notice, but you will also create a positive vibrational energy around yourself. People will gravitate to you when you are vibrating on a happy frequency. Enthusiasm is contagious! I am sure you are a lot like me and would rather hire a happy, positive, enthusiastic person, opposed to a negative, complaining, or grumpy one.

Getting customers sometimes starts before people even know they need you. Say you meet someone in a store checkout line, and you begin talking about your business. Let them know how happy you are to serve and help the people in the community and that you would be happy to help them if ever they needed you. Be joyous! Make them fall in love with you and want to hire you even though they may not need you yet! Genuinely express how happy you'd be to help them. Simply leave a good impression, along with a business card—never leave home without a few in your pocket!

If your main method of reaching prospective new clients is via the phone, then getting the customer starts with that first call. It's important to share and express that happy-go-lucky attitude through your phone conversation without them ever having laid eyes on you! That's why putting a smile on your face before answering the phone or calling a customer is so important. A person's attitude, what they're feeling or thinking, will not only affect their energy but will also affect the vibrational tone and frequency of their voice. If it happens to be gloomy, mad, or angry, then that is what will be reflected, and that is what the customer will hear. This will not serve your business. If you begin smiling and think "happy" before getting on the phone, regardless of what you may be feeling or what may be going on in your life, you'll reflect a happy, calm demeanor to the person on the other end of the phone by following this practice. This simple technique works every time!

Closing the customer begins when you show up with that same happy attitude. Present a confident personality, be courteous, friendly, and knowledgeable. Be willing to serve people and help solve problems. Speak from appreciation, and convey that you practice good work ethics and are a trustworthy company of integrity. Let them know you will go that extra mile for them; and do not be afraid to ask; what it is you must do, to earn their business!

DETERMINING YOUR VALUE

How will you know what to charge a customer? How do you determine your costs compared to the value that you'll give in exchange for your time, talents, and energy? Every type of business will have different rates. Each person has their own value and belief about what they're worth based on reasons like speed, details, or knowledge. A company's rates may vary for reasons based on their desire for expansion or what they want to accomplish for themselves in life. Your self-worth and reason for being in business can help to determine your rates.

You may want to create an additional income only so you can enjoy all of the benefits of the tax breaks a business owner receives. Or you may want an outlet to serve people while earning money.

Maybe your main objective is to work just enough to create a decent income for yourself so you can have quality time with your family. You understand that this creates tranquility within you and makes you a better person. Plus, you love being home when your children get off the school bus and being available for after-school activities, clubs, or events. Your main interest is having time for your family while earning a good income!

You might as well work at a faster pace and plan to only work part-time. Or you might be the entrepreneur who wants to earn thousands a day and hire employees to help you accomplish that goal. It's your business; the choice is yours. No way is right or wrong. It's simply what works best for you.

I loved working part-time. It allowed me the opportunity to make good money while giving me the freedom to have quality time at home and be there for my kids when they got off that school bus. In fact, all the kids in the neighborhood came to my house after school, where I was waiting with a healthy after-school snack recipe for us to make together. We actually had after-school hangouts down to a science. While one kid would be making the Kool-Aid, I'd be teaching the whole group how to make the healthy snack, which we did together. It was great fun for all of us. I actually became like a second mom to many of the kids in the community, and many still refer to me as their second mom to this day.

Being self-employed allowed me to be in charge of my life. I was able to be home for my kids and participate in after-school activities. I was able to create a better life for my family. Having my own business even allowed me the free time to become the Boy Scout leader for my sons' troop and the Girl Scout leader for my daughter's troop. I even had the time to assist the youth pastors on Wednesday night church services. Self-employment gave me the freedom to do the things I wanted to do and live the life I wanted to live!

Determining your worth and what you should charge your customers are valid questions to ask when going into business. To know how much is appropriate, you would estimate the labor and material cost of the work or service you provide, this will also depend on the type of business you have chosen to be in. This will require some research on your part in order to make an intelligent decision as to what you will charge compared to others doing the same type of work in your community.

If you're choosing to be in a service type business, such as an electrician, plumber, handyman, or pool cleaning, etc., then you'll most likely estimate your work by what is known as a service call. This means you will charge a standard flat rate to visit their home or business, and that would include performing a certain amount of work for that fee. As an electrician you might charge $125 for the first 30 minutes to diagnose and fix the problem, but if it wasn't fixable in that amount of time, then you would charge an additional $125 per hour starting after the first 30 minutes, plus the cost of material used.

As a pool cleaner under a monthly contract, you might charge $250 to clean a customer's pool every week and include supplies like chlorine. If a filter or pump needed to be replaced, then you could charge a service fee of $75 per hour for your labor plus the cost of the material, including an upsell fee for supplying it.

This is where your research will prove beneficial in determining what the going rates are in your type of work field and in your community.

"We make a living by what we get, but we make a life by what we give."
- Winston Churchill

STUDY YOUR COMPETITION

Take notes on your competition. Learn what they're doing to keep their business running profitably. How are they advertising or promoting their work? MOST IMPORTANTLY, what are they charging? One of the ways you can find out is to act as a potential client and call or email a few of your competitors to inquire about their fees and services. Ask each of them the same questions and keep notes on each business. Once all of your research is completed, contrast and compare each company. This will help to give you a better understanding of what you should charge and the best ways to operate your business.

SAMPLE CONVERSATION WHEN CALLING YOUR COMPETITION:

Hello! My name is (make up a name), and I'm calling to get an estimate.

1. Do you give free estimates?
2. What is your service area?
3. Do you charge by the hour or by the job? If it is hourly, ask for their rate.
4. How much is your weekly, bi-weekly, or monthly rate?
5. Do you have a minimum number of hours required?
6. How do you schedule your clients?
7. How busy are you?
8. Are you insured or bonded?
9. How long have you been in business?
10. Are you offering any first-time customer discounts?
11. Do you offer written information about your company's service, policies, or   procedures that you could send me?

12. Do you have a mission statement?
13. What are your payment options?
14. Do you accept credit cards?
15. Is the work done by company employees or by the owner?
16. Do you supply the materials?
17. What type of discount do I get if I supply my own materials?

After the phone call, make an actual appointment to get an estimate from them. Ask for a written estimate and study what it includes. This will help you to compare each company and the service that they provide. Ask about procedures and any other questions that you may have.

QUESTIONS TO EVALUATE YOUR COMPETITION:

1. How did they answer the phone?
2. Were they polite?
3. Did they listen to what you had to say?
4. Did they answer all of your questions?
5. If you left a message, how long did it take them to call you back?
6. When they came to give you the estimate, were they prompt?
7. Were they polite?
8. Were they happy to be there?
9. How was their appearance?
10. Were they knowledgeable and know what they were talking about?
11. Did they leave information about their company?
12. Who gave you the estimate, the owner or employee?

Document your answers on each company's evaluation sheet. Doing this will give you a wealth of knowledge and will better equip you to be ready once your business is up and running.

PRACTICE MAKES PERFECT

When starting out in any business, none of us are perfect. Our perfection comes from experience. Depending on your type of business, you may need to practice your skills prior to your company opening its doors. If you can practice your services with a family member or a friend, then do so. Begin perfecting your skills. Remember: Practice Makes Perfect! As you work, evaluate your work performance and look for ways to improve your work or services you'll be providing. Then ask yourself what another company would charge to do this same type of work.

SOME QUESTIONS YOU MIGHT ASK TO EVALUATE YOUR WORK PERFORMANCE:

1. How long did it take to prepare for the job and get to the job location?
2. How long did it take to get the job done from start to finish?
3. Was time managed well?
4. Did any of the tasks take longer than estimated?
5. Was there any time wasted while servicing the customer?
6. What can be done to improve job performance next time?

Answering questions similar to these will help you to evaluate how long it takes you or an employee to complete a job. This will help you find places for improvement in your practice.

SCHEDULING

As a business owner, you'll soon discover there is always work to be done. You may even find that you're always working. Taking days off to take care of yourself or your family may seem impossible! There just doesn't seem to be enough time in the day to get it all done. Although that statement may hold some truth, it doesn't have to be true for you! Yes, the work will always be there, and you may even feel that you can't stop until it's done, but that's not such a bad thing. The key here is to create a good working schedule where you can utilize your time wisely and efficiently. You're building your life's dream, after all, so, keep your eyes on the prize and follow a precise schedule. I can promise you it will give you more time and fulfillment in your life!

You want to be around to enjoy the fruits of your labor, so you must take time for yourself and those you share your life with. The key is to structure and balance your time. You must create a schedule with you and your needs in mind. Scheduling your time in business and your life is number one and will be the most important thing to maintaining balance. A clear, written schedule with your needs and goals will ensure that you maintain organization and productivity in your personal and business affairs.

The purpose of a schedule is to manage your time. Everything you plan to do should be written down and organized with the date and time the events are to be done. Best practices dictate that your tasks must be written out and followed until they are completed! Operating your business using a well-organized schedule will prove to be profitable! This practice should become a personal and business ritual for you to follow daily.

> *"If it's written down, it will get done."*
> **- Tammy Mihalic**

THINGS TO CONSIDER BEFORE SCHEDULING:

1. How many jobs or hours can you work in a day without wearing yourself out and while still maintaining a high level of service?

2. If your business requires you to be at a job location, then travel time should be considered when you schedule a client. Remember to schedule work in the same area on the same day and think about your transportation time getting from one job to the next. Food breaks and fueling up your car should be estimated in your schedule as well.

3. When scheduling, always be sure to organize your clients in geographical order. This will save you a huge amount of time. Map out your week by the location of the area (north, south, east, west), then geographically schedule your customer for that area. Consider your time to travel to the area and to each scheduled job, and most importantly, the time to get the job done.

4. Think about the extra time you may want to give yourself in the schedule for getting from job to job. If you allow yourself an hour to get from job to job and it takes only 20 minutes, you'll be wasting time! A 15- to 20-minute window buffer should

suffice. If you feel the need to space your jobs out with more time between them, then do what makes you feel more relaxed and in control. To maximize your revenue, keep in mind that jobs may require a tighter schedule.

5. Take time to eat. Keep snacks readily available. Snacking will help keep your energy level high. If you don't have any energy, you won't feel much like working. Depending on your schedule, you may need to set aside a solid mealtime and relaxation period for 20 to 30 minutes. Some people are content with eating between jobs, while others wait until the end of the day to eat. Think about what will make you the happiest, and make it a part of your work schedule each day.

6. Don't forget about your day-to-day errands and appointments, things like picking up supplies, banking duties, dental appointments, or accounting needs. These things will need to be incorporated into your schedule too. You can designate one day to take off for this or have an open hour or two during the day for such activities.

7. Schedule in your administrative work, both business and personal. This will help you stay on top of your payable and receivable accounts, filing, record keeping, opening and responding to mail and emails, returning phone calls, etc.

8. Have a plan for dealing with setbacks that could occur in your schedule like car failure, getting sick, or some other unforeseen emergency. Be sure to put this plan in writing in your service manual. Show consideration by contacting your client immediately if a change were to occur in your schedule that would affect them. Keep their contact information readily available.

"Good fortune is what happens when opportunity meets with planning."
- Thomas Edison

What will determine your value? What are you worth?

_____

_____

_____

_____

_____

_____

_____

_____

_____

_____

_____

_____

_____

_____

_____

_____

_____

_____

_____

_____

_____

_____

_____

_____

_____

_____

_____

11

UNDERSTANDING YOUR CUSTOMERS

Getting to know your customer and understanding their needs and wants is an important part of any business. The more you know about your clients and their expectations of you and your service, the better equipped you'll be to serve them. Besides knowing your clients' needs, wants, and expectations of you, try to get to know them personally, and remember their name. This will be especially important if you're operating a small business that requires you to see your customer regularly.

Plus, find out and record things like their birthdays, anniversary dates, or religious preferences and keep it marked in their file. Don't forget to save them on your calendar so, when they do come up, you'll be reminded to either wish them a happy birthday or send them a card or email for that special day.

Putting that extra touch into your business dealings will go a long way toward keeping your clients happily connected and loyal to you. Let them know you value them as a person and a customer. Leave them feeling that you care. This practice is the best way to establish and keep new clients.

Making a client or any person feel special is a reward on its own. A vital ingredient in any entrepreneur's endeavors is to establish trust and credibility with those they are working with. Make them feel comfortable with you and your work. Genuinely be interested in them, always have a good demeanor, and wear a smile. A smile is powerful, and goes a long way. Just imagine all the ways to build long-lasting customers and friendships that'll ultimately build your livelihood.

Customer Service Essentials

1. Be courteous and friendly.
2. Make your customers feel important.
3. Build a business friendship.
4. Listen to your customers' needs.
5. If you don't know, then ask. Never assume an answer.
6. Do the work you were hired to do. Give 110 percent.
7. Make every customer feel like they are number one.
8. The customer is always right—unless you have proof to the contrary in writing!

A happy customer will spread the word to others who are looking for the same dependable and exceptional service. Take the time to know your customers. Laugh with them. Know their personal interests. Enjoy their company. Be genuine. Show that you care about them. Always share a joyful smile and a friendly conversation; this builds customer loyalty.

"Delight Your Customer."
- Warren Buffet

As with any business, there will be times that you may encounter a difficult customer. Not everyone who hires you will be pleased or satisfied 100 percent with your services. Don't be offended if it happens; just stay calm and listen to their concerns. Oftentimes, it's simply a misunderstanding that can be easily fixed. Even though it doesn't feel good when someone is not happy for whatever reason, just stay calm, listen to them, repeat back their concerns so that they know you heard them, then let them know that you're willing to fix it! Remember, we're all human with our own opinions and expectations. Though it may feel difficult having any type of confrontational conversation with a customer, be open to listening and STAY CALM! Apply understanding to the problem, and fix it if you can. Remember, it's only a part of doing business, so don't sweat it. It's nothing personal.

"If you change the way you look at things, the things you look at change."
- Dr. Wayne Dyer

By putting everything in writing, you can avoid creating a difficult customer. Have the service you'll be providing and the cost written in black and white, and then have both you and the customer sign the contract (and possibly a witness, depending on your business type). This will confirm you both are in agreement and understand what services are provided and paid for.

Depending on your type of business, estimates should not be given over the phone. You must always see a job or plans to estimate a job properly. You will also want to meet your potential customer.

When giving the estimate, take notice if that customer tends to complain about things in general. If they're complaining about people or how people work or do things, you can assume that they'll also, be complaining about you. Complainers are usually people who are never satisfied, no matter what you do for them.

The critical customer is another warning signal that could lead to a potentially difficult customer. If they're verbally expressing criticism about another hired company, they'll most likely criticize your work too. If you do discover that you have a critical customer on your hands, try to counteract their criticism by exchanging words that are uplifting and positive. By doing this, you'll keep good energy around you and will have the potential to sway them to be positive.

The "I-want-it-for-free" customer has the potential to become a difficult customer, especially when you don't oblige! This should be addressed in your contract that everything above and beyond your written scope of work will be done for an additional fee, not free. I know you're thinking, well, if it's easy, then why not? Well, when you do one thing for free (unless it's for a promotion), you'll soon be asked to do another and another. This can lead a customer to a place of expectancy, and when you tell them you can no longer do this for free and must charge a fee, they'll get mad. This could then lead them to dismiss your services. Keep boundaries when it comes to working for free. Remember, you're in business to make money!

The customer who is never satisfied: Some people will never be satisfied no matter how well you do the job. Sometimes these people are simply looking to get something for free, or they have such high expectations and demands that no one could ever meet their standards. A customer who is never satisfied will usually not remain a customer for very long no matter what you try to do to satisfy them. So, don't be offended if they suddenly say, "I no longer need your services." Simply say, "Okay. Thank you and goodbye!"

The customer under contract who doesn't pay on time is the most difficult of all customers because they affect your bottom line! How and when you are to be paid should be written into your estimate and your service manual. This estimate should be signed by you and the client receiving the bid. Let it be known that you collect payment upon the completion of each job or within a 30-day period (or whatever your established payment terms are). From experience, once a customer gets 30 days behind on their payment, you're actually taking a chance on not getting paid at all. The reason is simple. Your bill will become one of their cumulated debts, which will make it harder for them to pay off. Don't be a bank! You're running a business and you must get paid.

I think we can all agree that it's not always easy dealing with difficult people. The key here is to remember to stay calm, let them know you understand, and be cordial when dealing with them. Remember, it's only business! DO NOT TAKE IT PERSONALLY. Normally, it's a really simple fix. So, stay calm and show no negative emotions. Negative emotions could get you into trouble. If you find you can't solve the problem or situation, then you may need to simply break the contract and let that client go.

"Excellent customer service is the number one job in any company! It is the personality of the company and the reason customers come back. Without customers there is no company!"

- Connie Edler

What ways can you create better customer relationships?

12

CLIENT SCREENING

Screening your client when they call is very important for both you and your potential customer, especially when operating a service type business. This is for your own safety and security. You wouldn't want to ever walk into a situation that could put you in danger. You need to get to know your potential customers well enough by screening them with a few basic questions before ever visiting their home or place of business to give them an estimate.

While screening the potential customer, you'll also have the opportunity to offer information about your services, which is why they called you in the first place. While offering information about yourself and your business, make sure to ask all the appropriate questions to that prospective customer. You'll ask the same routine questions to every potential client who calls you, including getting to know a little bit about them, how they found you or if anyone referred them, what they need help with, the job address, their name, and their number before going to their home or place of business to give them an estimate. Getting all of their information on that initial phone call is most important.

The screening of a potential customer begins at the point of your introduction. Always make sure you answer your phone with a positive mindset and a happy smile on your face. Yes, that is what I said: a happy smile! Put a happy smile on your face before answering your phone or returning a phone call. Your positive mindset and happy smile will actually vibrate through the tone of your words and will not only keep the conversation pleasant but will also, generate an overall feeling of well-being with your customer!

I've been answering my phone this way for years. Whether it's a personal or business call, it really does make a difference to the people receiving the call. It's no different than if you answered the phone with a mad scowl on your face. It would generate a negative emotion, and that negative emotion will vibrate a tone that will also come through the words of your introduction, and it could give your potential customer the feeling that they're not being valued or that they are a bother to you. You definitely don't want your potential client feeling that way because you could lose them as a customer!

Remember, first impressions are what people recall about us. So, make it count, make it matter, right from hello. After you have your mindset in a positive place and a smile on your face, then say hello, state your company's name, followed by your name, then ask, "How may I help you?" For example: "Hello! Golden Touch House Sitting, Sally speaking. How may I help you today?"

Never just say, "Hello." Say more than that. Be engaged. The key is to engage your potential customer, or whomever you may be talking to, right from the start. When engaging customers, we show we care. It makes them comfortable and gives them the feeling they know us.

So, keep them engaged! This little secret will help you land more customers and keep them.

You've answered your phone. Now what? Well, now the conversation for a more thorough screening can begin. Always ask for their name and write it down immediately; you don't want to forget their name halfway through your conversation and have to ask again. Make sure to always have a tablet and pen available prior to answering your phone or returning a call. Jot down the time they called and the time you plan to call them back. This will keep you orderly.

Next, ask for their phone number and address of the job location. This will, of course, be determined by what type of business you chose to go into. Followed by their work needed. You'll need to ask also how they heard about you. This will help you to determine which advertising is working best. Jot it down next to their name. If your referral was from a person, you'll want to make sure to thank them! Whether you thank them by text, email, phone call, or a simple thank you card by mail, make sure to thank them. It will go a long way and could lead to more referrals. Always express gratitude to those who help you.

As you are gathering and writing down information about them, be sure to offer information about yourself. It's always better to give the information before they ask. It shows you're efficient and organized. Take charge of the phone conversation. Let them know what services you offer and how long you've been in business. Express how you love to help your customers and how you enjoy adding quality and value to their lives. Let them know that serving your clients is your number one priority!

When the client brings up pricing and asks how much you charge, the business you've chosen to be in will determine how you answer that question. If you're a service business where each job has a different cost based on job specifications, then you'll want to see the job and not give a price over the phone.

If the customer insists on knowing a ballpark idea of what you may charge before coming out, simply say, "I'm sorry, I cannot give you a fair price until I see the job." Express that you value them and wouldn't want to mislead them. Express the importance that, in order to accurately estimate and provide a fair price, you must see their job first. Politely ask to set up an appointment to give a proper estimate. Meeting the customer face-to-face increases your chances of getting the job!

"You never get a second chance to make a first impression."
- Andrew Grant

SCREEN IN PERSON

Now that you are at your scheduled appointment, you can continue your customer screening process. Not only will you be able to see and evaluate the job, but you'll also be able to get to know that potential customer, and they'll have the opportunity to get to know you. Having that one-on-one time with a potential customer will increase your chances of landing the job, or you may decide you don't want their work. This is another reason why you'll want to make arrangements to meet in person.

Keep the good impression going at your appointment by arriving on time! When you arrive promptly at your scheduled appointment, you are showing the potential client that you value them and their time. It displays responsibility and a good work ethic. It gives the client the sense that you'll make a good candidate for the job they are looking to hire someone for.

A clean appearance is a must. Do not arrive dirty or smelly. A potential customer will find that offensive and won't care to invite you into their home or place of business for an estimate, much less to do work for them on a regular basis. Make sure your shoes are clean, too, or have booties to wear over your shoes when entering a person's home. The key is to always be clean and presentable. Be attentive to your customer's needs. Get to know them. Ask and answer all of the questions pertaining to that job. This meeting is the time to be transparent about your company and to land the work.

Arrive in a clean automobile. When a vehicle is trashed, it signals that the owner is too busy or just doesn't care about appearances. To a customer, that might mean those same ethics will flow into that person's work practices. I know you probably think they won't see your car. However, what if they liked you so much so that they walked you to your car after your appointment? Then what? They'll see your car, and if it's a mess, it could potentially ruin everything you just worked for. Having a clean car will also be better for your morale. So, just do it!

"Imagine your customer is your best friend—listen to their concerns, be a shoulder to lean on and then shift the focus from what went wrong to how you can help make it right."
- Rachel Hogue

What questions will you ask to get to know your customers?

_____

_____

_____

_____

_____

_____

_____

_____

_____

_____

_____

_____

_____

_____

_____

_____

_____

_____

_____

_____

_____

_____

_____

_____

_____

_____

_____

_____

_____

13

INCREASE YOUR REVENUE

ADD A SERVICE

You're now in business, and things are going great, but you feel led to have more. Now you must begin to think of new ways to increase revenue in your business. You can increase your revenue by adding a new service to your company's menu of services. The key here is to analyze your company and see what will return the most profit without creating an overbearing workload or expense. Work smarter, not harder.

When adding additional services, look for a service that can be easily added to your existing business type. For example, if you have a house-sitting service, you could extend your services to include pet sitting. You would charge per pet visit. This could be done while house sitting or separately. At each visit, you would take their pets outside for 15 to 30 minutes, feed and water them, clean up any pet messes, and make sure the home is safe and secure when leaving. This could be done once or twice a day or as needed by the customer.

Important - Always know and understand how to do all the services that you're offering the public. <u>NEVER CLAIM TO KNOW HOW TO DO SOMETHING WHEN YOU DO NOT!</u> If it's an unfamiliar field that you want to be involved in, then simply get acquainted and qualified with the procedures of that field.

USE PROMOTIONS

People love the word FREE. So, use it! Use the word *free* to make your new customer feel special. When we get something for free, it causes a happy feeling to arise inside us. Not only will you be giving something away for free, but also creating a happy feeling inside another person. This is a good thing. Be generous as an individual and as a business, and the rewards will come back to you—guaranteed! It's the law of reciprocity, and it works! Remember, giving goes a long way! Be generous with yourself and your business. Give back.

Here are a few promotional ideas you might use to get more work when building your company:

1. Offer a free service after your customers buy a certain number of services. Or get a free product after buying a certain amount of products or services.
2. Give a free gift to your first-time customers along with a note saying, "Thank You, I appreciate your business." This is an inexpensive way to show your gratitude toward your customers. Don't forget to mention that your free gift has no cash value. This means you will not be giving cash in exchange for them not accepting your free gift.
3. Give a 10, 15, 20 percent discount on a future service you provide. This will give the customer the incentive to hire you again in the

future. This discount could be mailed or emailed with a thank-you note and a discount certificate or code. This discount should be applied to future work only and have an expiration date. The expiration date will encourage your customer to get the work done now. This also is a great holiday promotion to use.

4. Advertise a 5 percent discount for future use, for referring five clients who actually hire and pay for your services.

5. My favorite promo of all is the Cash-Back offer. The Cash-Back offer applies to customers who give you active referrals. This is when you give the referring customer cash back for all referrals who actually book, use, and pay for your service. (The Cash-Back offer should specify the minimum amount of service the referral must pay for in order to qualify for the offer.) You could apply it to a current customer by giving them cash back on every ten services purchased, for example.

Here's how it works: say you offer a $20 Cash-Back on every tenth service. After you have serviced them ten times or have a confirmed, paid, referral, you would actually pay them $20 in cash.

I know you're probably thinking you'd rather barter with them and offer a service for free, which is fine when starting out. However, the Cash-Back offer actually works in your favor as a business owner. Here's why. When receiving the full payment for a job, it's documented in the gross income earned section, which looks good on your company records. Your Cash-Back offer is labeled as a company expense, which then lowers your net income, which means you will pay less in taxes. Plus, let's not forget the revenue that was created from those new customers. So, it actually is a win-win for your company.

Promos are all about ways to market and promote all the services that your company has to offer. No matter what type of promotion you may offer, make sure it benefits the growth and financial well-being of your company. There are many ways to show appreciation to your new client and existing ones. Use my ideas or figure some out on your own. Then put them to use!

"Giving goes a long way.
Be generous with yourself and your business. Be
serendipitous!"
- Tammy Mihalic

What promotions can you think of to expand your business?

_____

_____

_____

_____

_____

_____

_____

_____

_____

_____

_____

_____

_____

_____

_____

_____

_____

_____

_____

_____

_____

_____

_____

_____

_____

_____

_____

_____

_____

_____

14

HIRING EMPLOYEES

Depending on your business, there may come a day when you will want to hire employees so, you can grow your business. Hiring additional help means you'll be able to service more clients and meet the needs of your customers more quickly and efficiently without having to do all the work yourself! Having employees will help your company grow to a level that will allow you to create a passive income. Meaning you'll be bringing in income by doing very little or none of the actual work. It was with the help of "hundreds" of employees that made it possible for me to grow my business to seven figures. When growing a business, you cannot do it all on your own. You must have adequate help!

"A building is not built by one brick alone!"
- Tammy Mihalic

Small Business owners are the number one contributor to employment in the United States and possibly the world over. This is how our economy grows and functions well! When we create businesses, we can create jobs that give back to our communities. When you hire that mom, dad, or student to help you get your work done, you are not only taking care of them, you are taking care of their families, or those they support. It is my favorite thing about hiring help! You are actually helping that person to provide for their family. It really is the best part about being a business owner. Small businesses are the heart of the American people! It truly is what helps our economy flourish while taking care of the majority of the American people and their families that they provide for!

If you plan to stay small—and there will be many of you who do—that's okay! You do not have to be anyone other than yourself. This is your life. Your vision. I know many successful people who either work alone or have only one employee, and they're completely happy. They are earning the amount of money they want to earn and are living the lifestyle they want to live, and you should do the same!

When you are ready to hire help, write out a list of the work you want help with. Be very clear about the duties you expect to be done. It's ideal to hire help who can be multifunctional and be a perfect complement to you. Someone who can do their job without you being there! Be very clear and up front about the position you are looking to fill when you're interviewing. So, if you were looking to hire an administrative assistant, you would let them know you want them to answer the phone, get the mail, pay bills, send out bills, run errands, schedule clients, clean the office, and do any other task you need done. Once you have found the right person to fill the position, an agreement should be written up with boundaries set in place, and their expected work duties you are hiring them for. Then the agreement should be signed by both of you. You will keep the original in their file and give them a copy.

If you haven't done so by now, you will need to get an Employee Identification Number (EIN). This is a government requirement to hire employees legally. (See Chapter 3: What is an EIN?)

For your convenience, here's the link to apply:
https://sa.www4.irs.gov/modiein/individual/index.jsp

As a boss, you must learn to delegate responsibilities, set boundaries, and make deadlines. Without boundaries, rules, and regulations, your employees will not be very productive for your business. Unproductive employees will cause you to lose money. You want your employees to work as efficiently as possible. Spend adequate time with them after you hire them, train them well, praise them and give appreciation! Employee development should always be priority number one!

As a business owner with employees, you'll need to stay involved in order to maintain good employee morale. A business owner who stays involved with their employees will generate loyalty, a better work team, and a more productive company! When the day comes that you hire an accountant to run your books, set strict rules. Stay involved and watch your money. Know what money is coming in, going out, and what it is being spent on. Do not add others to your bank account—checks should only be signed by you, not a signature stamp! Please! For your own well-being, remember to watch your money!

As a business owner, you are the manager. Additionally, keep your team motivated and bring out the very best in each of them. You'll want to encourage them to act as a team and work well together. Give them the feeling of belonging! Inspire your employees to feel as though they're family and that they are a part of its longevity and success, because they are! Offering a monthly or yearly bonus is another incentive to keep your employees motivated to work well.

When employees are inspired, the company's overall productivity increases and morale soars through the roof. It's important to maintain good communication at all times, even when situations are difficult. You want your employees to feel they can come to you about anything, anytime. Keeping an employee engaged will create honesty and loyalty for years to come, not to mention they will be your eyes and ears when you're out of the office or unable to be on a jobsite.

Once you have employees, you may be able to reallocate your time. Use this time to monitor your company's records, check in on jobs, reach out to customers, create more revenue streams, refine your marketing plan, or strategize your exit plan, because one day you may want to sell your business.

"Value your employees. They are at work the days you stay at home."
- Tammy Mihalic

HIRE AS 1099 OR A W-4 EMPLOYEE?

Once you have decided to hire employees, you'll need to decide how you want them documented in your books. As a business owner, you have two ways of documenting and registering your employees for the IRS. One, as an actual employee, and the other as an independent contractor.

When your company hires an employee, you are required to withhold state and federal income taxes as well as social security and Medicare taxes from your employees' wages. You are also required to pay a matching amount of Social Security and Medicare taxes for your employees and to pay state and federal unemployment taxes. Additionally, you will be required to purchase workers' compensation insurance. This will protect you and the employee if there were ever an accident on the job. Each employee you hire will be required to show proof of who they are with an ID or Driver's License and supply a copy of their social security number (SSN). This is how the government associates us with our tax contributions. They will also be required to fill out a W-4 Form (Employee's Withholding Certificate) that must be filled out before starting work. This records each employee's legal name and social security number and their withholdings and should be kept in your employee files. This form shows that you have engaged in a trade or business and are paying compensation to them. If they need an SSN, they must apply for one using Form SS-5, found on, www.ssa.gov website.

Form W-2 is required and will be completed by you. It needs to be filed with the Social Security Administration by January 31st of the following work year. This too must be handed or mailed to the employee by the same January 31st deadline. This form shows the employee's withholdings paid for that tax year. These forms can be obtained and filed through the IRS.gov website.

Filing and issuing a W-2 is something you can do on your own by filling out forms provided by the IRS and mailing them in. With the help of accounting programs like QuickBooks, you can file digitally. Programs like these are great for documenting all of your business income and expenses. Accountants can do this for you at a fee. Hiring a payroll service is another option for you when hiring employees. They normally charge a small percentage based on your gross payroll amount. It actually may be cheaper to use a payroll service than it is to hire an in-house-accountant to do your payroll and file the taxes. Do some research and see what works best for you.

Hiring workers as independent contractors means they'll be doing the work that you need done, but they'll be working for you on their terms, not as a regular employee. They are basically their own business, and you would pay them straight pay for their time worked as a non-employee. At the end of the year, you would issue them Form 1099-NEC, which reports independent contractor income. This is the easiest way to hire help, but your business must qualify. Normally an independent contractor is responsible for paying their taxes and providing their insurance and will be required to give you a certificate of insurance for your records. This certificate should be kept in their file and will need updating every six to twelve months. (Check with your insurance company to see if you will still need to buy workers compensations insurance on an independent contractor.) Depending on your business, you may want them to sign a non-compete agreement. This typically prevents workers from accepting employment from a direct competitor or from taking your customers from you.

An incentive for the employee to be an independent contractor is they're allowed to have tax deductions (cell phone, gas, insurance, car payments, registration, a home office, etc.), unlike that of an ordinary employee. As a 1099-NEC employee, they are basically their own business. (See IRS Independent Contractor Guidelines to see which occupations qualify.)

Remember that anyone you hire represents you and your company. So, it's imperative to screen any potential help thoroughly and check their credentials and references. A background check may be necessary, and your insurance carrier may require a drug test. Hire those who you believe will be disciplined to get the job done in a timely manner and will represent you well!

Before hiring a new employee, make sure they are aware of the company policies that will be enforced while working for you. Your policies should be written in an employee handbook that the employee must read and sign, confirming they understand and agree to your company's policies. One copy should be given to the employee, and one should be kept in the employee's personnel file to refer back to when necessary. These are protective measures to follow when hiring employees, so, if ever you had to fire someone over misconduct, you will have proof that they knew the policies and signed an agreement stating that they would comply.

"The smartest business decision you can make is to hire qualified people. Bringing the right people on board saves you thousands, and your business will run smoothly and efficiently."
- Brian Tracy

What characteristics will you look for and need in an employee?

_____
_____
_____
_____
_____
_____
_____
_____
_____
_____
_____
_____
_____
_____
_____
_____
_____
_____
_____
_____
_____
_____
_____
_____
_____
_____
_____

15

IT'S ALL ABOUT YOU

TAKING CARE OF YOUR PHYSICAL SELF

As I'm sure you can imagine, running any type of business can be emotionally and physically taxing on your body. Plus let's not forget about the stress that can come with it if you're a worrier! Regardless of your business type, as a business owner, it's important to incorporate self-care into your daily regimen. After all, without you, the job won't get done. Here are some easy basic ways to help you to take care of yourself:

1. The number one way to take care of yourself is by staying hydrated. Drink plenty of water throughout your day. Hydrate with eight glasses of water a day or more. If you work outdoors or your job involves a lot of physical labor, you'll require more water. Water keeps your brain alert, your body healthy, your joints lubricated, and your skin looking young. Don't like plain water? Try adding some freshly squeezed lemons, limes, or oranges. They have natural electrolytes and are full of vitamin

C. Another great hydrating drink is coconut water. Cut back on soda, coffee, and energy drinks.

2. Take breaks to stretch your body throughout your day regardless of your job type. If your job involves a lot of sitting, incorporate stretching and getting out of your chair regularly, also make sure to exercise your body at least three days a week. Take a brisk walk, dance, practice yoga, jump rope, lift weights, or go on a quick run. Just make sure to add some sort of physical workout into your weekly schedule. This is important because exercise causes the body to release endorphins, which elevate your mood, and keeps you strong and agile.

3. Take special care of your feet; they carry you to everyplace you need to go. Besides regular pedicures to keep your toes happy inside your shoes, try giving yourself a relaxing foot massage with oil or lotion after soaking your own feet in warm water with a bit of Epsom salt.

4. If your job requires you to be on your feet all day, wear properly fitted shoes that are comfortable and have a good sole. If you work on a construction site or in a manual labor job, make sure you wear the safest shoes for the work situation.

5. Watch how you lift and pick up things. Always use your legs, never your back, when picking items up. Never pick something up while twisting your upper body because this can cause your back to go out. Always pay attention to the movement of your body when picking things up.

6. If you use toxic or strong chemicals or solvents on the job, pay attention to how the products make you feel. If you notice that you're having any adverse reactions to a product, discontinue its use. Beware of multiple product fumes mixing in the air (this has the potential to cause dizziness or nausea or even death).

7. Take breaks regularly throughout the workday to curb fatigue. A few minutes to meditate on successfully accomplishing your task while inhaling deep breaths followed by stretching will do

the trick. Remember, when you don't make any time for yourself, it can cause burnout, which could lead to depression and lack of motivation to get things done. Always pay attention to how you feel. Keep your thoughts positive and happy.

8. Take time off. Don't work 24/7. Not only is it not healthy, but it'll also lead to burnout and can cause you to make bad decisions when you're overworked! So, schedule that lunch with friends or a day at the beach. Do something to reward yourself for a job well done.

9. Eat healthy foods like raw fruits, vegetables, and nuts. Nuts, like walnuts, are a good brain food. Their oils are essential for your body. Almonds are excellent for heart health and full of antioxidants. Are you always on the run? Try drinking raw smoothies with added vitamin supplements blended in to keep your body operating at its optimal best.

10. Listen to music. Musical vibrations help to keep your state of mind elevated. Choose your music wisely and keep it playing softly in the background if possible. It will help to keep you motivated and calm.

11. Sleep is required by the human body to function at its optimal best. Six to eight hours nightly is needed for good health; aim for that. Restorative sleep helps you think more clearly when having to make rational business decisions. Plus, overall, it helps to make you look and feel happy!

12. Stress-reduction techniques like seven-minute meditations, listening to soothing music, or reading positive affirmations are great ways to reground and recharge so you can rethink any situation you may find yourself in that needs a solution.

13. Exercise your brain by doing mental exercises that will contribute to better cognitive thinking. Games that involve solving puzzles, spelling, counting, or trivia are good for mental acuity and agility. Your brain is a working muscle machine and must be utilized and exercised daily!

QUICK, HEALTHY, ON-THE-GO FOODS

When you're on the go, it's wise to have readily available quick and healthy snacks that can be prepared in advance. Advanced preparation will almost always guarantee that you'll eat healthy snacks while on the run. This will keep your energy running high throughout your day while you work and will keep you away from junk food.

Here are a few things that can be prepared and packed in convenient portion sizes to have available in your refrigerator or freezer at all times. These are what I call fast food snacks. You can vary these for your individual needs or taste. The key is to keep your snacks simple and as healthy as possible.

1. Carrot and celery sticks
2. Mixed nuts or trail mix
3. Cheese sticks
4. Fresh fruit—apples, blueberries, strawberries, bananas, pears, grapes, peaches, plums, and nectarines—any kind of fruit will do.
5. Sliced watermelon, cantaloupe, honeydew, pineapple, zucchini, squash, cucumber, radishes, peppers, broccoli, or cauliflower
6. Humus and chips
7. Individual yogurt cups or sticks
8. Individual sized peanut butter cups. Peanut butter goes great with a variety of fruits and vegetables. Peanut butter spread over a celery stick and covered with pomegranate seeds is amazing. It even goes great with carrot sticks or apple wedges. Vegetables and fruit are a better alternative to only crackers and peanut butter.
9. Prepared, cooked chicken or beef strips. Bag in portions sizes and leave them in the freezer until you're ready to use them.

10. Premade and frozen quesadillas—either cheese, chicken, beef, or vegetable—are a great snack to make in advance and taste excellent cold or hot! These can be stored in the freezer until needed. Don't forget to add a premade guacamole or salsa cup.

11. Baked sweet potatoes, hot or cold. They make great baked potato chips that can be prepared in advance.

12. Bottled water, juice, and teas. (No soda.) These can be frozen and taken out the morning of use. Plus, they make great icepacks in your lunchbox.

13. Premade vegetables and fruit smoothies are great frozen and will thaw into a nice cold, on-the-go drink to get your energies flowing for an afternoon pickup.

14. Homemade baked kale chips with Parmesan cheese or cheddar and your favorite spices can be premade and packed for an easy on-the-go snack.

15. Nut balls are an excellent grab-and-go healthy sweet snack. Simply combine until smooth your favorite nut(s) along with raisins, ginger, butter, or coconut oil, turmeric, and cinnamon in the blender, then roll into balls, put into snack bags, and refrigerate. They are delicious!

16. Dates stuffed with almond or cashew butter and a walnut.

17. Boiled eggs also make the list. Not only are they easy to make in advance, they are a healthy on-the-go snack, full of protein.

These are just a few of the many fast and healthy snack foods that you can keep prepared in your refrigerator or freezer and have ready for when you are on the go. There are so many healthy things that can be made in advance to save you time. Be creative and make up some of your own ideas. Just keep it healthy!

"Feel better, work better."
- Lailah Gifty Akita

What are some of your favorite healthy habits and snack ideas?

16

FINAL WORDS OF INSPIRATION

As a growing entrepreneur, I worked many long, exhausting hours to earn my piece of the American Pie. Occasionally, I found myself working over 80 hours a week just to keep up with all of the work, and that was even with hundreds of employees! On several occasions, I worked over 72 hours straight without sleep. How I did it was by the grace of God. This could happen to you too. You could even experience the feeling of wanting to give up. I know there were times when I felt like giving up, but I didn't! I didn't know how to quit, and I didn't want to learn how! I pushed through those limiting thoughts and kept telling myself I can do this! My motto was *I can do all things through Christ Jesus, who strengthens me!*

Whenever I felt overwhelmed, I realized I was trying to do everything on my own and was failing to seek God's help with my decisions! After that analysis, I sought God's help with everything I did. Then suddenly, my life got easier. I began to effortlessly land huge high-paying jobs that allowed my company to expand and earn more money. It was very exciting! So, if or when you ever feel discouraged, have hope, and look to your Creator for help and direction. *Follow your intuition and walk in faith regardless of what you may fear! Choose faith over fear! Just remember; we may plant and water the seed, but it is God who gives the increase! - 1 Corinthians 3:7*

Wealth-making possibilities are available to us practically every day. All we have to do is consistently look for them. Be present in your everyday life. Take notice and be aware of moneymaking opportunities and seize them. Make it a practice to take notice of the needs and wants of people in all areas of their lives. Look for ways to make people's lives better, more practical, and easier. How could you increase their quality of life or solve a problem? This kind of inquiry is the mindset of a creative entrepreneur!

As an entrepreneur, always strive to be a better version of yourself. Stay fresh. Stay educated. Keep up with the times. Discipline yourself. Wakeup early. Take care of yourself, exercise. Get plenty of sleep. Maintain good work ethics. Keep your integrity. Be open-minded, kind, and considerate. Take chances, and don't be afraid of calculated risk! When one takes risks, one finds great rewards!

Risks are a part of this whole economic game we call life! Life is more than just a fun board game with fake money and pretend wealth and fame. We are living a real life, with real consequences, real hurt, pain, and suffering. There is no Get Out of Jail Free card. We're playing with real money, real property, and real lives! You must be serious about your business, your money, your investments, and the lives you affect! Unlike the board games, you need real money to win!

Maybe you didn't have control over winning the board game, but I am here to let you know that you are in control of winning in your own life. You can have the properties that bring great passive income! You can have the business of your dreams! You can be that self-made millionaire! You can be the one who creates a financial empire of wealth! *By utilizing the secrets of the rich, you can earn your own piece of the American Pie!*

You can be a great contributor to the betterment of humanity. You have the ability to build financial stability, not only for yourself but for others too! Life is more than just fun and games. If we lose our home or our investments, it's more than saying, "That was a fun game. I'm glad I played. Maybe I'll win next time!" No. In real life, you don't lose fake money; you lose real money—real money that you've worked hard for. Humans need money to make this world go around. Without real money, you can't buy your dream home, car, motorcycle, or boat, much less have the means to take care of yourself or your family or send your kids to good schools, go on a vacation, retire, leave your legacy, or help someone else.

As an entrepreneur, you know that taking risks is necessary to get ahead in life, and with those risks comes great reward! Entrepreneurs are disciplined and walk in great faith! We choose faith over fear! We take the risks necessary to propel us forward to get those things we want in life. We believe in ourselves, our ideals, and our dreams! We trust in our intuition, and our decisions, knowing we will reap our reward if we don't give up.

What I hope you take away from this book is an insight into all of your possibilities for living an abundant life, learning how to capitalize. I want you to know that you can do anything you put your mind to. You really can! Even when those things put your faith to the test. Have tenacity like a bulldog! Be determined! Hold on to your vision! Believe in your dream! Walk boldly and remain focused on the outcome! Be a brave thinker and action taker! Persevere through challenges! Hold on to your integrity! Stay aware of presented opportunities and be open to their possibilities. *Seek, and ye shall find. Knock, and the doors will be opened unto you!*

If you grow weary, don't give up. You become what you think about, and scripture says it best in Galatians 6:9: *And let us not be weary in well doing: for in due season we shall reap, if we faint not.* That means you become your thoughts, and if you don't give up, you will succeed and receive the reward of that image you hold in your mind, and feel in your heart. What image are you choosing to see for your life? Make it matter! Make it count!

As you play the real game of life, let your focus remain on winning. When you sat down to play Monopoly for the first time, you didn't sit down with the thought that you were going to lose. You came into the game with the intention of winning. Treat your business the same way. Keep your thoughts and intentions on winning, stay persistent, move forward, take the right action steps needed, and you will win.

Seizing opportunities and going into business for yourself is a lot like getting the Get Out of Jail Free card! That's because as a business owner, you create financial freedom for yourselves and those you love! You get to live a life of abundance with the certainty that you will always be financially free!

"Remember to keep in mind that every business is a service that is scaled down to a person's personal interests, needs, or wants!"
Tammy Mihalic

Those interests, needs, and wants come in many forms. Take, for example, in 1933, during the Great Depression, people were desperate and needed inspiration. People needed to be happy and laugh again. Americans needed diversions and ways to forget their problems for a while. America and her people needed hope for a new and better future.

Charles B. Darrow saw that need and took an already invented product from 1903, the Landlord Game by Lizzie Magie, and reinvented the game. Darrow created the game we all now know as Monopoly. He added complicated rules that required some study before you could play. Like many games, you had to roll the dice and play with game pieces that kept you going around and around a board until one last player was standing.

The objective of Monopoly was to buy and sell real estate while erecting houses and hotels, along with trading, mortgaging, and making deals to earn money. The game ends when one player after another goes bankrupt until there is only one player left. People came to love the game and found it to be inspiring. It allowed people to not only laugh again, but to fantasize and dream about winning in real life. The game gave people hope of actually having money again and owning property. It excited and motivated people to believe in a new and better future.

Darrow pursued his passion for this board game and eventually got the interest of Parker Brothers, one of the nation's oldest and well-known game manufacturers in America. In 1935, Parker Brothers, feeling this game was a godsend, purchased the rights to the game, and it went on to become a huge success and still is to this day. Parker Brothers believed that it was a success because it was the right product at the right time. Darrow, however, never created another game after Monopoly and retired raising cattle and orchids. Darrow won the game of life, earning his piece of the American pie, and dying a millionaire in 1967.

Another motivated entrepreneur was John H. Johnson, an Arkansas native, who found himself living in Chicago, where he graduated high school with honors. As an advocate of Dale Carnegie's book *How to Win Friends and Influence People*, Johnson soon came to realize that others just like him had aspirations for a better life. They, too, were seeking opportunities to enter mainstream society. They, too, were interested in knowing more about politics, culture, social life, the general public, their community, and all of the things it had to offer.

Having a journalism background from working as an editor on his high school newspaper, Johnson landed the opportunity to work at Supreme Liberty Life Insurance, where he eventually helped publish their company newsletter.

While working at Supreme Liberty, he came to realize the needs of the African-American people and decided to create a magazine patterned after *Reader's Digest*, naming it the *Negro Digest, which later became Black World.* Using his mother's furniture as collateral, Johnson borrowed $500 to organize Johnson Publishing Company. While having permission from Harry Pace, the president of Supreme Liberty Life Insurance, to use their mailing list, Johnson mailed out 20,000 solicitations for subscriptions at two dollars a year and much to his surprise received 3,000 responses. Within that year, the magazine reached a circulation of 50,000 subscribers.

Eventually reaching a circulation of over 150,000, the magazine soon became an important voice for striving African-Americans. This confirmed Johnson's view that there was a large, literate, African-American middle class, and they, too, were hungry for stimulating articles of common interest and news in their community. Johnson then pondered to himself that if this magazine was doing so well based on the idea of *Reader's Digest*, then why not a magazine about life?

With this insight in mind, *Ebony* magazine was born. *Ebony* was a glossy picture magazine devoted to articles on Black middle-class life. The magazine featured news of interest to the striving community and success stories. Along with fashion trends, entertainment and culture. *Ebony* would also publish a list of accomplished influential Black-owned and operated companies. Every issue would contain one or more articles on the subject. The first issue of *Ebony* was released in November 1945, and within days the press run of 25,000 was sold out.

It all started with acknowledging a common interest among the people and the community where Johnson lived and then taking action on his vision to fill that need. Imagine that. Something as simple as creating an informative magazine became his business, bringing value to others and huge success to himself.

I am sure many of you have heard the name Mary Kay. Mary Kay is a multi-level marketing cosmetic company created for women by Mary Kay Ash. Mary Kay Ash loved the idea of women having beautiful skin and knew how important it was for them to have their own money. As a working woman, she knew the difficulties women had in earning an income in the male-dominated workplace. She experienced first-hand the struggle as a single mother trying to take care of her children while having to work one or two jobs. She understood how hard it was for women to get ahead in the corporate world and still be a good wife and mother.

As a single mother, Mary Kay, found herself having to work while raising three kids under the age of eight. Mary Kay went on to work for Stanley Home Products in Houston, Texas, where she sold products door-to-door, or held home parties.

One night, while holding a home party, she discovered the hostess was a cosmetologist who had been working on her own skin care cream. All of the ladies attending were friends of the hostess and had been using her product for months. This cream seemed to make the women's skin look flawless and beautiful. At the end of the Stanley party, the hostess sent everyone home with her products to try. Mary Kay loved the product so much that she became a regular customer.

Not long after, she left Stanley to take a sales position at the World Gift Company in Dallas, Texas. There she created a marketing strategy, using sale incentives, to encourage salespeople and customers into action. However, once again, she found her career path blocked from going any further in the executive world due to her sex, so she resigned.

Out of her discouragement, Mary Kay drew up two lists. One list covered what was wrong with companies dominated by males. The second list showed how to correct those things and make the workplace more sensitive and aware of the needs of women and working mothers. From these lists, a dream company for women was created.

Knowing exactly what to sell, she sought and bought the formula to the cream made by the cosmetologist she had met years earlier while working for Stanley. That cream would become the foundation of her company, Beauty by Mary Kay.

Mary Kay's successes were largely due to her entrepreneurial skills to see opportunities and to take action on them. She also was brought up with the belief that she could do anything, taught to her by her mother! Plus, she was excellent at giving love and praise. She always imagined people wearing a sign saying, "Make me feel important," and she made that a practice with everything she did; along with giving lavish gifts, like the Pink Cadillac, to all those consultants who qualified with high volume sales that worked for her. Out of her desire to help women to become more financially independent, Beauty by Mary Kay, was born in 1963!

Another entrepreneur whose business skyrocketed due to his inquisitiveness, is marketing genius, Ron Rice. While working as a lifeguard in Daytona Beach, Florida, Ron was gifted a free trip to Hawaii. There, he noticed the Hawaiian women cracking open young green coconuts and smearing what he calls, gel copra oil that was inside the coconut, all over their skin as a sun protector. He was fascinated by this, because he had never seen that before. When he returned to work, Ron began thinking about his future, and what he was going to do with his life as he was looking out over the beachgoers, ensuring everyone was safe. As he continued to ponder his future, Ron took notice of the families having fun playing in the water and sand, as he noticed the products the women were spearing all over their hot skin. This scene made him remember the Hawaiian women using the gel copra as a sun protector. And that's when the idea hit him—why couldn't he make a natural suntan oil using the same coconut oil as the Hawaiian women used? So, having studied chemistry at the University of Tennessee and having taught it for seven years, Ron used his chemistry knowledge and began to formulate his idea!

Ron made his first batch of suntan oil in a big metal trash can, which he still has to this day, using a broom handle to mix his natural oils, and different fragrances in his garage where he bottled and labeled the product himself. Having discovered the idea from the Hawaiian women is how the product got its name, and that is how Hawaiian Tropic suntan oil was born! Established in 1969.

Ron tested his newly created oils on the people he protected while lifeguarding at the beach. This product testing allowed him to find out what people liked and wanted in a suntan oil. Not only did they love his oil because it glided smoothly over their skin, but he discovered that his unique selling proposition was the scent. It was the tropical coconut scent that was making the sale! *Smell sells!* People loved the way his product smelled over his competitors' products.

In order to generate sales, Ron began to solicit all of the beach goers and those sitting alongside hotel swimming pools and the local tourist shops to stock his product. His perseverance paid off, and soon his product was being carried in a number of local stores. However, there was one store owner who owned two of the hottest tourist shops in the area who just wouldn't budge. This store owner wanted nothing to do with this new oil until one day, Ron came up with a grand marketing strategy.

Ron approached some tourists and offered them a whole summer's supply of his suntan oil if they would go into this particular store to buy their tourist gifts and also request seven bottles of Ron's suntan oil! The girls were happy to help. Upon checking out, they asked the clerk for suntan oil and pulled out the empty bottle Ron had given them to show the store owner so, he would know what they were looking for. They handed him the bottle, and one of the girls said, "I want seven bottles of THIS oil, Hawaiian Tropic Professional Tanning Oil!"

The clerk said, "I don't carry that brand." The girl replied, "Well, that's the oil I want! I guess I'll have to go find it at another store," and left.

Well, as I am sure you've already guessed, that consumer demand caused the store owner to immediately order the product and start carrying Hawaiian Tropic Suntan Oil in both of his stores. This was a pivotal moment for Hawaiian Tropic and for Ron Rice, the inventor.

That strategic move helped land Hawaiian Tropic in all the stores in the area, later landing distribution in stores across America and eventually the world. With hard work, dedication, and determination, Hawaiian Tropic went on to generate over four billion dollars in sales!

After successfully running his business for 38 years and creating a legacy for his family, Ron decided to sell his company and retire. However, forever the entrepreneur, in 2016, Ron came out of retirement and created a new skin care line with his daughter, Sterling, called Havana Sun Suncare Cosmetics.

When I interviewed Ron, he was very generous with his business advice. Here are a few business takeaways Ron would like to share with every reader looking to go into business for themselves or to create a product. *Work hard for what you want. The harder and harder and harder you work, the luckier and luckier and luckier you'll be in your business. There is no substitute for hard work. When you work hard for your business, your business will work hard for you.* Ron believes in doing everything right. *Be honest, because it's the greatest thing you can do! Don't cheat. Run a clean operation. Keep clean records. Pay your taxes. Have fun with it, and enjoy what you are doing. If you make a claim, then let it be right. Look around and do some research around your business interest. Make your business unique, one that others don't have. Most importantly, pick the right business for you, and be the best business that you can! As Ron puts it, "Have the better mousetrap!"*

As you can see, these businesses didn't just fall out of the sky, and neither will yours! Every day you must work toward your dream. You must work hard to make it happen. Work hard at polishing your skills.

Make a conscious decision to take at least one action step every day toward completing one goal. That first step forward creates momentum for your next step, your second step! Every step brings you closer to that vision that you see in your mind! Nothing moves until you do. Discipline yourself to stay focused. Don't put off to tomorrow what you can do today. Be committed to the end results. Get it done!

You may even want to consider creating a vision board to help you visually stay focused on your goals and dreams! A vision board is a collage of images and statements that represent the things you desire and the goals you want to accomplish. If used properly, it will help you stay focused on your desired outcome while stimulating your mind into action. I once put a picture of Hawaii on my vision board, which was a trip I could win if I reached $25,000 in sales within that year! I did even better than that! I manifested two luxury trips to Hawaii! Having faith, and feeling as if it was already done, is how I brought my vision to pass, and that is how you will too! Keeping the faith, and feeling as if it is already done, is how you will bring your vision into reality!

The Lord said it best to the prophet Habakkuk 2:2-3: *Write the vision; make it plain on the tablets, so, he may run who reads it. For still the vision awaits its appointed time; it hastens to the end and it will not lie. If it seems slow, wait for it; it will surely come and it will not delay.*

Trust in your power of pursuit. Trust in your vision. Trust it will come to pass. Reach for what you want. Place your trust in action. Take action on what it is you must do to get to where it is you must go. DO NOT GIVE UP! Persevere in faith! See your dream business and life as already being fulfilled! Remember, someone needs you to show up and to be on your A game.

Celebrate your "small wins" every day. Keep a record of these wins for encouragement. Operate your daily affairs with active, open mindfulness. If you ever find yourself discouraged, don't talk yourself into the negative of "I can't." Talk yourself into the positive of "I can." *I can do all things through Jesus Christ who strengthens me! Speak life over yourself!*

You become what you think about. Did you know that most limitations are self-imposed? So, don't limit yourself! Live happily. Stay positive. Be grateful. Cherish the opportunities that have presented themselves to you, and let it show. Shine! Life was meant to be an exciting adventure. Every morning you should leap out of bed with enthusiasm and excitement because you have a business to run! Choose to live a life full of happiness. Be alive. Design your life by doing what you do well. Realize success will come if you progressively keep pursuing your notable ideas. Live on purpose and stick with it. Do not allow anyone, including yourself, to stop you from attaining the vision that you see clearly in your mind's eye. You can do this!

Write each goal on an index card. Include the start date and the date you wish to complete it. Keep them with you to look at and read every day. If you write it down, it will get done! Any conceivable thing you put your mind to will manifest, provided you stay laser-focused, feel your worth and take action, which is key.

Remember, you become what you think about! So, watch your thoughts! If you see them going into a negative place, quickly shift them back to positive, and see yourself happily accomplishing your goals! Keep your goals lingering in your mind, 24/7! Give of yourself more than ever before! Realize your purpose, and stay persistent with a burning desire to succeed in bringing your vision into reality. Keep your attention on your dream. Look in the mirror every morning at the start of your day and say to yourself, "I have what it takes. I am doing this! My success is absolutely guaranteed if I don't quit! I am a disciplined successful prosperous business owner!" If you need a subtle reminder, write the words on a note next to your bed or mirror. Reading statements like these will remind you of who you are.

Create a list of your "Must-Dos" and then ask yourself; What action steps must I take to get what I want in my life while maintaining my integrity? What type of person could I be that others would want to emulate? What legacy will I leave behind? Do this for both your personal and business affairs. Make a conscious effort to get clear on what you want and how you plan to play the game of life to ensure that you win in it!

Business opportunities are everywhere. All we have to do is look for them and seize them quickly. We regularly are presented with things that people or businesses in our community need, and these needs can easily become a business if we take action to make it so. Recently, while visiting some friends, I had the opportunity to cook for them and share my culinary skills and recipes. My friends thought my recipes were over-the-top and loved my cooking so much that they asked me if I would cater their next work event. Without hesitation, I said yes.

Right there, I found myself with the opportunity to possibly create yet another business, a catering service. With a BIG smile on my face, I began to imagine the different types of companies that could also benefit from my services. Who else would enjoy my food? How would I go about finding my customers, and which ones should I seek? Then I asked myself what other kinds of businesses would hire a catering company? How could I market or encourage them to hire my services? The thoughts came flooding in about what a catering service would look like for me.

As a caterer, you are more than just a person who delivers food to a party. You must have people skills and know how to communicate with people on several levels. You must receive and execute orders gracefully from the hosting customer and from fellow staff or other hired help—and let's not forget the guests. You'll need to know how to cook for a large number of people. This is really quite simple to figure out. Just take your favorite recipe and multiply it to reach the number that will be served. You'll need to create menus and shopping lists. You'll have to learn serving and serving sizes, and you must know how to shop and cook according to the number of people who'll be attending the event. You'll need to be organized and efficient with your time. Time-management is a must! A caterer is required to work according to the time schedule and agenda of the person who hired them. The customer is the one who determines your schedule and sets the time they're going to eat. As a caterer, you must also comply with health codes and regulations. Those were just some of my thoughts I had as I processed how to create a successful catering business.

Without going into great detail, do you see how easy it is to spot business ideas? All you have to do after that is take the initiative and get it started. Follow the same process as I did with your business idea. Write everything down that pertains to it. When you're ready, refer back to this book to guide you easily through what it takes to make your business legal. Here's to your success!

"Seek and ye will find!"
- Matthew 7:7

BONUS: MONEYMAKING BUSINESS IDEAS

How many businesses can possibly be created? Well, the number is limitless because people have an endless number of wants, needs, and desires that need to be satisfied. If there is a need, then eventually, there will be a business to meet it. People want services that will enrich their lives and make their lives easier. What product or service could you provide to your community that would make their lives better? What services can you do well enough so, that people would pay you good money to provide? Observe the world and the things that are in it! Look for possible ways to make improvements and enrich the lives of others, and you could discover your new business!

If you've been reading this book and are still contemplating what business might be a good fit for you and your skill set, I've created a list of some of the many business ideas that you can run from the comforts of your own home, and some of these you can do right from your computer. Keep in mind that some of these businesses will require additional skills or education beyond high school to operate legally, but you could still operate them with the help of a licensed qualifier. Do consider educating yourself in a construction trade! Yes, this requires advanced training and experience, but many of the trades pay very well, and these jobs are always in high demand, which will keep you in business. The main purpose of this book is to simplify and outline the process of setting up, organizing, and structuring your own business while encouraging you to reach for your dream so, that you, too, can earn your piece of the Great American Pie, and leave your legacy behind!

In this list, I have **highlighted in bold** the businesses that are easy to start and are in high demand. In fact, some, like, Home Care Service, could grow so quickly, that you may need to hire employees, right away. To fulfill the ever-rising need of helping elderly people who are choosing to live at home. Opposed to living in a nursing home or assistant living facility! This is a need that is very real and is never going away. The main qualification you need is the desire to help people live a quality life at their own home. Basically, you do for them the things that they use to do for themselves, such as cooking, cleaning, organizing, running errands, grocery shopping, helping with baths, dressing, changing bed linens, washing clothes, reading, playing games, taking them places or to appointments, or just being a kind-hearted companion to them. Each client will have different needs. What is nice about this business is that often times the customer is qualified for assistance through their social security and Medicaid will pay for your services. Do not confuse this with a healthcare provider. That is an entirely different business and is paid by Medicare. (More on that in another book!)

I do plan to write a series of how-to books showing just how easy it is to start some of these businesses. So, please, join my email list for updates at: www.tammymihalic.com

BUSINESS IDEAS FOR YOU:

1. Accounting Service
2. ***Assistant Living Home Service***
3. Adventure Tour Guide Service
4. Air Duct Cleaning Service
5. Aluminum Siding Installer
6. Antique Dealer
7. App Developer
8. Appliance Installer, Repair Service
9. Appraisal Service
10. Aquarium Care Service

11. ***Art and Crafts Camp or Classes For Kids / Adults***
12. ***Art and Crafts Instructor – Group or Private Teacher***
13. Artificial Turf Installing
14. Artist Service – Artist For Hire
15. Authorpreneur
16. Auto Body Repair Service
17. Babyproofing Home Service
18. ***Babysitting Service***
19. Baker or Dessert Making Service
20. Barn Building Service
21. Bicycle Repair Service
22. Birthday Party Planner for Children or Adults
23. Blacktop Pouring Service
24. Bookkeeping and Administrative Assistance Service
25. Bounce House Rentals
26. Bricklayer / Masonry Service
27. Bridal Concierge Service
28. Building Contractor
29. Business Planning Service
30. Cabinet Maker / Installer
31. ***Candle Maker Service***
32. Car Detailing Service
33. Carpentry Service
34. Carpet Service – Cleaning, Dying, Installing
35. Carrier Service – Personal or Business Deliveries
36. Catering Service
37. Chauffeur / Taxi Service
38. ***Chef / Cooking Service***
39. Chicken Coop Building Service
40. ***Childcare / Daycare Service***
41. Childproofing a Home Service
42. ***Children's Fitness Camps***
43. **Children's Birthday Party Planner**

44. ***Children's Daycare / Summer Camp Service***
45. Children's Transportation Service
46. Chimney Cleaning Service
47. ***Cleaning / Janitorial Service for Interior and Exterior***
48. Clock Repair Service
49. Closet Installer Service
50. ***Coaching Service – Life, Fitness, Business, Health, Dating***
51. Computer Programmer, Training, Repairs Service
52. Concrete Service – Staining, Stamping, Forming, Pouring
53. Construction Trade – Plumber, HVAC, Electrician, Framer, Etc.
54. Custom Tailoring Service
55. Demolition Service
56. Dietician Service
57. Disc Jockey (DJ) Service
58. ***Digital Media Conversion Service***
59. Dog Daycare / Dog Boarding / Dog Hotel Service –Your Home
60. ***Dog or Pet Grooming Service***
61. ***Dog Poop Yard Cleanup Service***
62. ***Dog Walking / Dog Sitting / Dog Training Service***
63. ***Drone Service – Operator for Photography, Repairs, Trainer***
64. Dry Cleaning Pickup Delivery Service
65. Door Installer Service
66. Dwelling Inspector Service
67. ***E-commerce Store Owner, Designer, Developer***
68. ***eBay Assistant or Seller Service***
69. ***Editorial Service – Copywriting, Proofreading, Editing***
70. Electronics Repair Service
71. ***Errand Service***
72. Event Planner Service

73. **_Fitness Instructor_**

74. Financial Advisor Service

75. **_Fix and Flip Homes – Buy Homes, Restore, Sell_**

76. **_Flea Market Vendor – Sell Whatever Goods You'd Like_**

77. Fence Installer or Repair Service

78. Freelance Digital Marketer

79. Furniture Maker

80. Food Truck Service

81. **_Food Delivery Service_**

82. Garage Door Installing Service

83. Gate Installing Service

84. **_Gift Basket Service_**

85. Glassblower Service

86. Golf Club Cleaning Service

87. Graffiti Removal Service

88. Graphic Arts Designer Service

89. **_Grocery Shopping and Delivery Service_**

90. Gutter Cleaning or Installer Service

91. Hairdresser Service

92. **_Handyman Service_**

93. **_Home Care Service / Home Health Care Service_**

94. Home Entertainment Installer Service

95. Home Inspector Service

96. House Sitting Service

97. House Staging Service

98. Hospital Bill Auditing Service

99. Ice Cream Truck Service

100. Insulation Installer Service

101. Interior Decorating Design Service

102. Inventor

103. Lamp and Light Fixture Repair Service

104. Land Grading Service

105. Landlord – You Own and Rent Your Living Space

106. Landlord Service – Bed-and-Breakfast or Airbnb
107. Landlord Management Service – Manage the property of others
108. Landscaping Design Service
109. Laundry Cleaning Service
110. Lawn Care Service
111. Limousine Service
112. Locksmith Service
113. Jewelry Designer / Repair Service
114. **Junk Hauling / Removal Service**
115. Makeup Artist Service
116. Management Service
117. Massage Therapist Service
118. Marketing Consultant
119. Medical Delivery Service
120. **Menu Planning Service – Online Business**
121. Mobile Car Washing and Detailing Service
122. Mobile Locksmith Service
123. Mobile Mechanic Service
124. **Mobile Pet Grooming Service**
125. Mortgage Debt Reduction Service
126. Moving and Shipping Service
127. Musical Instructor – Piano, Guitar, Drums, Vocal, Etc.
128. Musical Instrument Repair Service
129. Nail Technician Service
130. New Mother Infant-Care Home Service
131. Organizing Service – Residential or Commercial
132. Packing Service Company
133. Painting Service
134. Paver Installing Service
135. Pesticide Treatment Service
136. Pet Chef and Bakery Service
137. Personal Assistant Service

138. **Personal Chef**

139. Personal Courier Service

140. ***Personal Driver or Taxi Service***

141. ***Personal Fitness Instructor***

142. ***Personal Shopping Service – Groceries, Clothes, Etc.***

143. Photography Service

144. Physical Therapist

145. Piano Repair Service

146. Plant Watering Service – Indoor or Outdoor Plants

147. Playground Building Service

148. Plumbing Service

149. Porcelain Repair Service – Bathtubs, Sinks

150. Pottery Making Service

151. Power-Washing Service

152. Private Investigator Service

153. Property Manager Service

154. Real Estate Broker / Agent Service

155. Roof Installer Service

156. Screen Enclosure Installer Service

157. Seamstress / Tailor Service

158. Self-Defense Instructor Service

159. ***Senior Citizen Home Companion Service***

160. Septic Tank Cleaning or Installer Service

161. Shed Building Service

162. Snow Removal Service

163. Social Media Consultant Service

164. Stone Installer Service

165. Swimming Pool and Jacuzzi Cleaning or Installing Service

166. Tax Consultant Service

167. Teacher –Teach Skills or Hobbies You Know

168. Tile Installing Service

169. Tile and Grout Cleaning Service

170. Tour Guide Service

"Life is like a movie! If ever you don't like anything about it; rewrite your script!"
- Tammy Mihalic

Recently, I became a part of another great business that you might be interested in too! This is a "Perfect" business opportunity that can be ran from your home, and operated all over the world. A business that will not only make you healthier, but will help others in your family, and community to get healthier too!

No sign-up fee - No quotas - No inventory - No annual renewal fee - No geographic limitations - No storefront - No employees - Multiple ways to earn - Commissions processed daily - Unlimited income potential - Highest quality products - Ability to provide free samples - Recognized industry leader - Solid product warranty - Top quality marketing material - Easy financing - Incredible team support

SUCCESS HAPPENS WHEN TIMING MEETS OPPORTUNITY! Being in the right place at the right time is important, but taking action and seizing that moment is the next step that many people fail to do. If you are open-minded and keep your career options open and are willing to check out a legitimate opportunity, do yourself and your entire family a favor and take a close look at Enagic, the amazing Kangen Water from Japan. There is no denying that water is a hot commodity right now. People are discovering just how vital water is to health and life. One water in particular, Kangen Water, is making waves around the world. This incredible water is trending and the water ionizer industry is booming.

People are discovering the truth behind bottled water and they are looking for healthier, less expensive and more environmentally friendly alternatives. This shift in consumer awareness and demand has created perfect timing for this business. We are able to make the best water in the world, for pennies, and we are able to give it away for free, so, people can experience it for themselves. In fact, that's the secret to our marketing success. We give people free water. Once they feel the difference proper hydration can make, they want to own a machine so they can drink it right from their own system and give it to their family and friends. It's a formula for success that is working wonders in the lives who partake of it.

Founded in 1974, Enagic is a very successful, privately held company headquartered in Japan. During the last decade they have expanded aggressively around the globe including throughout the United States, Canada, Europe, Mexico, Russia, Malaysia, Indonesia, Korea, Philippines, and most recently into India. Enagic has been providing powerful business opportunities for people from all walks of life to join with the industry leader and help introduce and market Kangen Water all around the world.

The distributor compensation plan is so unique, it has actually been patented. As a distributor you are rewarded with direct commissions and sales overrides ranging from $285 to $1710 on the sale of every SD501, the company's number one selling machine. The potential is absolutely massive. Once you fully understand the compensation plan, you will realize why this is one of those opportunities you do not want to miss.

For more information about this business, please feel free to contact me at, www.tammymihalic.com

"Change Your Water, Change Your Life!"

As an individual, it is always important to find ways that you can give back. When we do this, we receive more in return. It is like your investment into life. It could also be looked at like a farmer planting seed in the ground at springtime who will reap a harvest in the fall. It's called, the Letter of Reciprocity! If you are not sure who you could give to, here I have presented a wonderful non-profit organization who is in the business of helping women to rise-up and be all God called them to be. You can read more about them here in this letter from the CEO, Claudine McDaniel, herself.

BEYOND CONQUERORS MINISTRY

The mission of Beyond Conquerors Ministry (also known as Beyond Conquerors, Inc.) is to bring love and hope to women who have been knocked down by life's difficulties by motivating them to rise again and pursue after their dreams.

Beyond Conqueror's Ministry, is a faith-based, non-profit, organization with educational programs for women who are single, widowed, divorced, separated from their families, or those who are facing domestic violence, poverty, divorce, financial problems, job disruptions, chronic illnesses, abuse, separation, loss, and even those in shelters. Through these programs, the Ministry seeks to help them realize their strengths, value, and self-worth. The Ministry incorporates in its programs teachings, coaching, and counselling to help the women find helpful ways to get back up again.

For more information please visit,
https://www.beyondconquerors.org/

To support women in adversity, please click on the link below to make your donation,

https://www.beyondconquerors.org/make-a-donation

You can also write to us at, info@beyondconquerors.org

Thank you so much, and may the Lord bless you!

Claudine McDaniel

CEO of Beyond Conquerors Ministry

Listed here are some of my affiliates I work with, and their free gifts, or trainings, that can benefit you. Including the OptimizeUpsell information for Shopify Stores. I hope you find them useful. Enjoy!

Do you want to discover expert secrets to selling physical products online and build your own ecommerce Empire? Learn how with this intense online training with Adrian Morrison, a top authority in the eCom space. For your Free training video and Special Bonus "$20K ECOM Secrets" a book that shows you how to build your own profitable eCom Business. Follow this link here to learn more: https://mcrmgo.com/go/appesa/3383 Plus, if you make a purchase, you'll qualify for a $100 rebate. Send purchase information to: www.tammymihalic.com to qualify

For those who create an online Shopify Store, you will definitely want the "OptimizeUpsell App." It will automate upsells on every product on your store for maximum profits. To read more about this use this link: https://mcrmgo.com/go/ouappp/3383/123 If you make a purchase, you'll qualify for a $50 rebate. Send purchase information to: www.tammymihalic.com to qualify

Do you want to learn a fun way to manifest all of your dreams? Then you'll want to get your FREE e-book, "Power Life Scripts" written by, Peggy McColl, to help you with that! Follow the link here to receive your Free copy: https://go.peggymccoll.com/powerlifescript-ebook?affiliate_id=2286925

Do you want to learn how to write your own book and use it as your business card? Many business owners do just that. When a business owner writes a book, it shows that they are an expert in the field of work they are in, and will give the customer confidence in

210

hiring you. A book also makes a great marketing tool! You could also become an Authorpreneur, and make writing books your business. To learn more about becoming an author, follow this link to your FREE Video: https://go.peggymccoll.com/prosperousauthor?affiliate_id=2286925 if you do signup, send me your purchase information to www.tammymihalic.com to receive a $50 rebate.

Do you want to hire a professional Freelancer to help with startup task like building your website, designing your Logo, or building and operating your social media accounts? Then you'll want to create a free account at Fiverr! There, you will find all of the help you will need for your business. You could even hire a Virtual Assistant (VA) to help you with your day to day operations, and so much more! Follow this link here to find inexpensive, qualified help for your business needs: https://fvrr.co/2PwlBU0

Once you're in business, you'll want to start Email Marketing, to create more business. Follow this link for a Free account, with unlimited emails: https://moosend.grsm.io/tammymihalic9219

Do you want to discovery how you can build a 6-Figure Digital Product Business? Then you'll like SamCart. Follow this link here for your FREE "10 Step System" Training Video: https://checkout.samcart.com/referral/10-secrets/HLGTd5x82vpGsdTY

Do you want to grow your sales and save time with automation? Or have a convenient way to keep your contacts together, while sending out and tracking marketing emails? Then you may want to try the program Keap. To check out their FREE Video, and see if they can help with any of your business needs just follow this link: https://keap.grsm.io/money-automation

Enjoy a beautiful, healing "Sound Bath" that effortlessly washes away all of the "Energetic gunk" and negativity that's been holding you back! This "Miracle Tone" was created based on REAL science; something called "Cymatics" (or the study of sound frequency). Follow the link here to get your FREE MP3 download. https://hop.clickbank.net/?affiliate=tammz&vendor=manifmagic&pid=gift2&tid=eypbook

As a business owner you may need documents and forms to help you manage your business affairs. Follow this link to find over 9000 Project Management Templates that will help you with those business needs. https://8c3ddje6ly8n1s19thj6qp18qb.hop.clickbank.net/?tid=EARNYOURPIECE

I thought some of you might enjoy the "Lost Book of Remedies" to help you take care of yourself naturally. Follow this link here to find out more about it! https://6b6c4nbl1n3kdr010lpeiork6l.hop.clickbank.net/?tid=EARNYOURPIECE

Do you want to learn more about real estate investing, or short-term sales? Follow this link here to learn more about this business. https://e4236si9ny8l7y5rpj2f9eqc3x.hop.clickbank.net/?tid=EARNYOURPIECE

To help you stay healthier while growing your business you may want this Plant Based Recipe Book. Follow this link here to see the yummy vegan recipes you may enjoy. https://543bdomgzk8ofrakvxyml92m8n.hop.clickbank.net/?tid=EYP

"When life changes, We then must change!"
- Tammy Mihalic

Keep this simple phrase in mind as you make your way in life with all of the adventures and changes it will most certainly bring.

I am truly happy and grateful to be divinely connected to each of you as you learn to capitalize in this "Great God Blessed Nation of America."

I thank you and wish you all well.

"Life is a game!
How will you play it?
How will you earn your piece of the American Pie?"
- Tammy Mihalic

Copyright © by Tammy Mihalic

Made in the USA
Middletown, DE
25 September 2022

11179990R00137